THE
7-MINUTE
SETUP

How to Achieve Your Business and Personal
Goals Faster and Easier

Frank J. Lopes

Read Page 2 Now!

**FINN-PHYLLIS
PRESS**

Book Cover Design by JetLaunch.net

Edited by Elizabeth Lyons

The 7-Minute Setup / Frank J. Lopes. —1st ed.

ISBN 978-1-7344043-6-4 (pbk)
ISBN 978-1-7344043-7-1 (eBook)

Contents

Introduction

The 7-Minute Setup method works. That's a bold statement, I know. But whether you're near the top of your game and wanting to advance or at the very bottom of a hole deeper than the Grand Canyon, The 7-Minute Setup works, plain and simple. All that's required is that you commit to it and actually do it.

The determination of how many feet deep in the earth your bottom sits or how far into the atmosphere your triumph hovers rests squarely on you and only you. The point when each person looks in the mirror and says, "How did I get here?" is different. In similar fashion, the point when a person begins to visualize, plan, and execute their ascension differs.

The perfect example of this is every single *Rocky* movie (except for *Rocky V*; True Rocky fans never admit the existence of that "movie"). In each film, Rocky has to overcome some type of adversity. Sometimes it's self-inflicted. Sometimes it's brought on by someone else. Sometimes it comes about simply through the circumstances life throws at him. Sometimes, it's a combination of two (or all three).

You may have heard of Chris Gardner, whose story served as the basis for the 2006 movie *The Pursuit of Happyness*. Chris navigated a challenging upbringing, to say the least. He was twice placed in foster care (once after his mother attempted to burn his stepfather alive), and his uncle, who was an important positive influence in his life, died when Gardner was only nine.

After enlisting in the Navy and being stationed in North Carolina as a medical corpsman, he took on a clinical research position at the University of California Medical Center in San Francisco. While he hoped to become a physician, he abandoned that dream after his girlfriend gave birth to his son, Christopher, Jr., recognizing how much financial and time commitment accomplishing the dream would require. As a lab assistant, he wasn't making enough money to support his girlfriend and newborn son, and one day he approached a stockbroker getting out of an extremely expensive car in a parking garage and asked him what he did for a living. For whatever reason, this man, Bob Bridges, took the time to meet with Chris over lunch to explain Wall Street and the basics of being a stockbroker. Further, he arranged meetings between Chris at some of the managers at large brokerage firms.

Chris was accepted into the E.F. Hutton training program, but that opportunity went south when the hiring manager was let go. Simultaneously, his girlfriend attempted to flee with their son, and Gardner was arrested after he tried to take Chris, Jr. from her arms and, as a result, she was swung into some bushes. After a week and a half or so, he was released from jail and discovered that his girlfriend had gone to the East coast with their son. Prior to his short stint in jail, he had befriended a broker at Dean Witter and had secured an interview for admission into their training program. He had nothing but a Members Only jacket and paint-splattered sneakers to wear, but he showed up anyway. He confided in the man interviewing him why he was wearing what he was wearing (though wisely left out the part of the story that involved being in prison for ten days).

After four months, his son's mother returned with Chris, Jr.—then two years old—and it was decided that the best place for his son to be was with him. The challenge was that the building Chris was staying in did not allow children. He kept his homelessness a secret from his employer and many nights had to choose between food and shelter. Those who saw the movie likely remember the scene when Gardner and his son slept on the floor of a bathroom stall at the BART station in Oakland. They also occasionally slept on BART trains. In short, he did whatever he had to do to support himself and his son while pursuing his goal.

One of the most notable figures in Chris's journey was Rev. Cecil Williams, who made an exception and allowed Chris and his son to stay in his church's shelter, which was exclusively for homeless mothers and their children. Rev. Williams continued to remind Chris that "baby steps count too," a simple but profound message that stayed with Chris. He often reminded himself that "baby steps count too" as he continued working toward his goal.

One of the best performers in his training program, he passed his Series 7 exam early, after which point he was heavily recruited by firms. He started his career at Dean Witter, where he was already known for his extraordinary work ethic. Ultimately, Gardner opened his own brokerage firm in Chicago, Gardner Rich & Company. By that point, he had welcomed another daughter and was able to move both of his children to Chicago to live with him. By 1988, he had earned over $1 million in one year and bought himself a Ferrari similar to the one that Bob Bridges was driving when they met in the parking garage.

Even before he knew that he understood, he understood that he simply had to find the "thing" he was incredibly passionate about (Wall Street) and keep going. He had to remember, probably hourly at times, that "baby steps count too." It took him fifteen years in total, but one baby step at a time, he got there.

That story—and others like it—always leave me wondering, "If they can do *that*, if they can overcome *that*, what can I do? More to the point, what *can't* I do?"

Of course, if my first and only answer was "become the starting shortstop for the New York Yankees at the age of fifty with zero experience in the sport," there's a reality-check component of The 7-Minute Setup method I'd need to factor in, and we'll talk more about that in a bit. But, in all likelihood, thinking too big isn't your greatest problem. Your greatest problem is that you don't have a plan or process on how to achieve your biggest goals.

Have you ever had one of those mornings when you had the alarm set for a certain time, but woke up, grabbed your phone to check the time, and realized it was a full thirty minutes before it was scheduled to go off? That's the way I feel as I begin writing this book. I simply cannot wait to share with you the method to make the rest of your life the best of your life. And it all starts with this moment, right now.

I don't know what time it is where you presently are. It's possibly only 6:30am, and you're just getting your day started. Or maybe it's 10:30pm, and you're reading this before calling it quits for the night. Either way, you might be thinking, "Yeah, Frank, of course I've got the rest of the day" or "Of course I have an entire day tomorrow that I can make the best of. Tell me something new." (Don't worry, I'm going to.)

Maybe you woke up in or spent the day in pain. Defeated. Burned out. Even if that's the case, the rest of today can be the best. Tomorrow can be even better. And the rest of your life can be the best your life has ever been. Because nobody starts where they ultimately end. Nobody.

In 2009, I was stripped bare. I had literally nothing more than I could carry from one place to another. The craziest part is, *that was only eleven years ago*! Big changes don't have to take two decades or twelve years or even two years. But the amount of time they *will* take is directly correlated with how long it takes you to get to 100 percent honesty with yourself about who you are and where you are as well as where you intend to go and how you intend to get there.

So, if you are not happy with the spot you're in right now, remember, even if you woke up this morning feeling broken, the rest of the day—the rest of your life—can still be the best it's ever been. That's what we're going to talk about—how you can get to that point as well as how I got to that point. I'm going to expose my own journey and be a bit vulnerable as I share some of my own experiences with you. It's going to be embarrassing at times. But my intent is to remind you that no matter where you are today or where you've been in the past, you can get to wherever you want to be.

I know you have goals. Everyone has goals. Your goal may be to earn $50 million over the next two years, or it may be to simply roll over and go back to sleep for two more hours. Either way, you have goals. None of this is about judging whether or not your goals are good enough or big enough—it's about whether or not you're able to efficiently turn them into reality before you're dead. Let me tell you something: In order to efficiently turn your goals into reality, you're going to have to incorporate a process other than the one you're currently using (the one that isn't working). Because, let's be frank here—if your old process were working, you wouldn't be reading this book. Now, if your goal is simply to go back to sleep, bookmark this page and take your nap. I'll be right here waiting for you when you wake up.

I know there are some people reading this who are on a clear, calculated mission. Fact: If you don't employ a proven method while on that clear and calculated mission, it will become less and less calculated as you begin the inevitable drifting we all become guilty of without a clear plan. And, if you drift long enough, there will be a morning, mark my words, when you will wake up, go to the mirror, have a look at yourself, say, "I have no idea how I got here," and throw up in the sink.

Have you felt that way before? I probably don't need to further describe it to you if you have. It's a feeling that's experienced frequently by some people—especially people in the automobile industry, in which I've worked for twenty-five years. Those of you in the industry may relate to this scenario: The end of the month arrives and you see your numbers, or an email comes over from the boss with the details of your monthly accomplishments. You look at the report, you absorb the reality of your efforts, which are right there on the report staring at you in black and white, and you wonder, "How did *that* happen?"

My goal is to make it so that you do not ever look at anything in your life from this day forward and ask, "How did *that* happen?" I want you to be in control. Having control of what you're doing is key. I'm going to show you how I took control of my own life, and how my method will work for you as well.

Yes, this is a book about setting business goals. But it's important that I set forth two crucial caveats before we go much further. One, your business goals don't have to include "run a ten-figure-a-year business" (or even a six-figure-a-year business). Unless you're independently wealthy (and even if you are), being clear about how you want to spend your time earning money (or managing your massive trust fund or investment portfolio) is of paramount importance to your overall satisfaction with life. Two, there is an interconnectedness between your career and six other key areas of your life—regardless of how invested you decide to be in any of these areas—that cannot be ignored. Even if you consciously decide that one of the areas isn't important to you, the fact that you're consciously making that decision is an integral part of the process. If you're consciously making those decisions, when someone down the line suggests that the missing piece of your success puzzle is the fact that you don't attend Mass three times a week, you won't waste a moment wondering whether or not you need to add that activity into your schedule; you'll simply and confidently declare, "I'm a practicing Buddhist" or "I'm an atheist."

Several months ago, I was driving from Seguin, Texas to Austin, listening to a podcast while driving on Texas Highway 123. Literally, that was the number of the highway. You can't get any more generic and rural than that. I kind of zoned out while driving—I was battling a cold, and my head was so congested that I couldn't hear out of one ear. I thought, *This really sucks. I would so much rather be doing anything other than driving on Texas Route 123 right now.*

I was suddenly coaching myself, saying under my breath, "I just have to push through." And then lightning struck the earth and I heard a deep voice shout, "But wait!" (Okay, the lightning and bellowing voice didn't truly occur, but it was a dramatic moment nonetheless.) I remembered in that moment that what

I was doing *wasn't*, in fact, pushing through. I was instead being *pulled* through. The entire reason I was in Seguin was that my Austin-based automobile dealership client bought a new dealership, and I wanted him to be successful. That called for an in-person meeting. And that fact, combined with my own long-term goals, were actually *pulling* me across Texas Route 123; I wasn't pushing myself through anything.

We spend so much of our lives "pushing" (or believing that we are). We say things like, "I don't feel well, but I have to push through" or "I'm short of my goal, so I'm going to push hard until the end of the month." We're always looking for more strength to "push harder" and more time to "keep on pushing." You know what? This mentality is completely wrong!

When you're pushing, you're applying force *against* something. You're making something go in a direction it doesn't want to go. You're forcing someone (or something) to do a thing they don't really want to do. This approach is especially bad when that someone being forced is you! Trust me, you're going to get sick of that eventually.

I used to constantly push. Every day, I'd get up out of bed and almost immediately start pushing. I'd pump myself up and, like Sisyphus, the cruel Greek god, felt like I was condemned to push that boulder (which was my life) up a hill, only to have it roll back down the hill at the end of the day. Sometimes, that rock would roll right over me on its way down.

Then, I stopped. I realized that it wasn't about pushing through; I'd had it all wrong. From that point forward, instead of forcing myself to push, I allowed myself to be *pulled*. I decided what I wanted my life to look like seven years in the future, and I let the magnificence of that vision pull me toward it. The life I chose to foresee was so magnificent and so rewarding that it had its own magnetic force, one that would wake me up from my sleep every morning half an hour or so before my alarm was scheduled to go off and pull me toward it. I figured out what I needed to accomplish over the following seven months, and I allowed those waypoint goals to pull me toward my ultimate goals. I set up a plan every week and religiously followed it as it pulled me toward success.

Rather than strenuously push through to the end of the day or month, I focused on my goals, dreams, and desires and allowed them to pull me toward victory every hour of every day. I didn't focus on the feeling of being unwillingly pushed; rather, I allowed myself to feel the sensation of being pulled. When you are operating based on the pull, you put tasks on your list because you know that completing them gets you closer to your goal, even if the to-dos themselves don't excite you terribly much in the grand scheme of things.

We choose to be pulled through life for many reasons. Perhaps if you *don't* choose to be pulled through, you're going to get yelled at by your boss (or worse, fired). One way or another, there's going to be some kind of negative consequence to not getting something done. That's where the pulling comes in—some days, you're pulled by your vision, and some days you're pulled by your strong aversion to the consequence of not doing something!

There was a time in my life when my momentum was created (and sustained) almost solely by the push. When I went back to work eight years ago after losing everything but the shirt on my back (almost quite literally), I had it in my mind that I was a huge failure. I had no perspective beyond "I have to push through" because I'd gone bankrupt and closed my advertising agency and restaurants. I then went back into the advertising industry, and before I had a vision beyond the simple "Don't mess anything up today," I had to push myself through each hour of each day until the clock struck five so I could head back home, grateful for another day successfully completed (without messing anything up).

These days, that is never my mentality. There aren't many (if any) things that I push myself through at this point in my life. I still work hard, put in long hours, and make daily sacrifices. But today, my dreams and goals painlessly pull me toward them. The long hours, hard work, and sacrifices are not forced; they're willingly undertaken.

Stop pushing your boulder up the hill, and start allowing yourself to be pulled by the view at the top of the mountain.

The people who employ The 7-Minute Setup—whether to radically change their life or to save a few extra thousand dollars or to simply get the pure-bred Pomeranian Box Hound they've been dreaming about for a decade—want the end result more than they *don't* want the pain involved in getting there. This approach works whether you're a high-level executive, an entrepreneur, a stay-at-home mom or dad, or a retiree. If your focus is family, your vision and plan will revolve around providing for them: grocery shopping, cleaning, doing the laundry, trimming the hedges so it's clear someone actually lives in the house, and so on. That's your work.

If you're seventy-five years old and you're considering how you want your life to look seven years from now, the first part of your vision is likely "I'm alive." If you've had a disagreement with one of your children, you probably don't want to die seven (or more) years from now, still engaged in that disagreement. If you've always wanted to be in a bowling league, I think it's safe to assume that you're not going to win the professional bowling tour, but perhaps you'll win the senior tournament at your local bowling alley. In order to accomplish that, you need to start bowling a few times per week. Maybe you'll hire a bowling instructor (do people actually teach bowling anymore or is that now a YouTube University course?). Maybe you'll quit smoking so that you'll have the endurance necessary to throw that twelve-pound ball down the alley several times during each practice. Whatever your 7-year vision includes, you can plug into it whenever you choose to and use The 7-Minute Setup method to make it your reality.

To be completely clear, I would never dare to tell you or anyone else what your 7-year vision—what you're being pulled toward—should be. This is why I said earlier that the career component of your vision doesn't have to include a ten-figure-a-year business. You don't have to envision yourself with rock-hard abs or phenomenal relationships with every member of your family. It's not about me telling you what happiness looks like in your world. It's about me giving you permission to define that for yourself and enabling you to set forth a process by which you can get there, understanding that there are seven areas that will directly or indirectly affect your ability to do so.

There are a lot of people who are happy exactly where they are, and that's great! They may think for a moment that they want more, because more always *sounds* good. Sure, you *could* make more money. You *could* be happier. You *could* be this and you *could* be that. It all sounds great until you look into it and discover what you have to do to get there. Then it's like, "Okay, I'm actually perfectly fine where I am."

Of all the people you've met in your life, there are undoubtedly some in the mix who are quite content with what you would call "mediocrity." They blame everything on everybody else when, in truth, none of it is anyone else's fault. The bottom line is, their vision is mediocrity. And they know it. Making $45,000 per year doesn't make one mediocre. Being eighty pounds overweight doesn't either. Nor does choosing to distance yourself from a toxic family member. But *resentfully* earning $45,000 per year at a job you absolutely hate, complaining each summer when you can't comfortably join the family beach adventure the way you used to because you've gradually packed on eighty pounds with daily trips to fast food restaurants, and continuing to grudgingly engage with Aunt Carol who does nothing but chastise you about your weight does.

Some people are just working wherever they work. They're pushing themselves through the day, and it wouldn't matter where they worked—whether at an advertising agency or an orthopedic surgeon's office or the Four Seasons or Target or the gas station (not a brand name gas station, one of those no-name ones)—because they haven't taken the time to identify what's pulling them. They're making the bare minimum that they need to pay the bills and live the mediocre life they've chosen to settle for. And if you get to the end of this book and employ this method only to determine that your truly incredible life seven years from today includes living paycheck to paycheck, feeling uncomfortable in your own skin, and engaging with idiots, then the method has still done its job.

But please, don't do that.

The just-mentioned generic gas station reference reminds me of songwriters who write country music. Honestly, they're the best marketers in the world. The country music industry is comparatively quite small, as is the automotive space, so I can relate. There are 17,000 new car dealerships in this country. There are another hundred thousand or so independent used-car lots. Each has an average of five salespeople plus all the people who work in the office and service department. The industry isn't tiny, but it also isn't as big as, say, the banking or pharmaceutical industry. It's also a very tight-knit industry. There aren't a lot of people within it who are very, very good at it, and those who are very good at it know one another, at least for the most part.

The country music scene is similar. The guys and girls who successfully write country songs release one, and almost immediately, every singer's agent wants the song for their client. All of these country artists clamor for the songs that are so good, written by a handful of elite writers, because they know that if they can get one of them, they're pretty much golden.

The reason for that is, country songs are all written *exactly* for the consumer. It's not like pop music from the '80s, which was written for the masses; country songs are, more or less, written for the guy (or gal) who drives an old pickup truck (preferably a Ford or Chevy), works in construction or a warehouse in East Tennessee, and consistently has issues with his or her significant other. While this may not be a popular statement, country songs are, for the most part, about being completely okay living a life of mediocrity. The only thing a guy can depend on at the end of the day, is his long-neck ice-cold beer.

Some of the people listening to country music, however, are on the fence about continuing to live their life in the same way. If one's vision is mediocrity, they're constantly going to be pushing themselves through everything. As Harvey Mackay says, "People begin to become successful the minute they decide to be."

The minute you must
part with disgust,
you'll make a change.

We choose to own the worst parts of ourselves—the ones that are *really* holding us back—only when we're ready and not a moment before. Not when Guru Greg says, "If you write such-and-such 518 times a week, you'll find your bliss" or even when we *appear* to be at our lowest low. Only each of us can decide when we're ready to stop digging the hole. And then, sometimes, we need to sit at the bottom of that hole for a while before we decide that we're ready to get creative about how to climb out.

The real key lies in teaching people how to be ready to start that climb sooner—not wait until they're in the depths of hell before they say, "Okay, fine, I have to change; I've really messed up." Because by that time, the person is already $80,000 in debt, surrounded by broken relationships and nothing even close to a six pack (unless it's the one they're drinking). The secret to getting people to really see their reality and take action toward something more exciting sooner rather than later lies in encouraging people to become self-aware far more quickly than we typically do.

The entire premise of The 7-Minute Setup is built upon a foundation of solid self-awareness and the speed with which one can turn on that awareness. It's not about a specific and rigid timetable (seven years, five years, two and a half years…) being applied to any and all goals. When I talk to people about building a business, I say, "I've been at this for eight years." But in saying that, I'm not telling them that it has to take *them* that long. If you pay attention to the steps I overlooked and the places where I messed up along the way, you can easily shave four or five years off the top in an instant. The determining factor when it comes to whether or not one does that is how long they're determined to do things their way and only their way. How long are they going to put off looking in the mirror and getting brutally honest with themselves about what they see?

There are also far too many outside factors at play for any one person to be able to say, "This took me eight years, so it will absolutely take you eight years." While you're living your life, the other people in your life (and in the world) are living their lives as well. Maybe you decided that you want to start a particular business on November 27, 2017, and at that time, there were three main competitors. But by November 27, 2019, there were nine competitors. There is no "This will take this exact amount of time"—even when we're talking about how long it will take for someone to look in the mirror and declare that he's not going to dig any deeper. That he owns the shovel and he's either been doing the digging or having someone else do the digging for him. And that he's ready to throw the shovel in the landfill, once and for all.

I have no right to tell you what your overall vision should look like. And I have only a very, *very* small right to tell you how to get there, and that's only because you picked up the book or otherwise asked me about this method. Tell me what your goals are. Whether I think they're big, small, lofty, or completely absurd, my opinion doesn't matter. You tell me what you want; I'll show you how to get there.

If you picked up this book randomly or found it somewhere, you're about to find out why. If you picked up this book because it was recommended to you or flat-out shoved into your hands by someone else, you're about to find out why. Regardless, it's time for you to stop making promises to other people. Stop saying, "I promise you that I'm not going to be in this job in a year." Stop saying, "I promise you that I'm getting out of this city." Further, stop saying, "I promised myself I wouldn't eat half an ice cream cake in one sitting" or "I promised myself I wouldn't skip my workout today."

Instead, start making *purposeful* promises based on your 7-year vision, and make them to *yourself.* That's what this book will enable you to do. You don't need to make promises to anyone else. If you don't keep the promises you make to yourself, the only person who suffers is you. Trust me, your family and friends are probably already suffering.

So, promise yourself that it's seven years from now. And the life that you're living is one that only you could imagine. Because, at one time, you did indeed imagine it. And you were the only one who could.

Now, let's get there.

Becoming More Frank

My parents came to the United States in 1967. They were both born in Portugal into very poor circumstances. My father was the second youngest of thirteen, and my mom was child number four of eight. At eight years old, my mother was forced to leave her family to become a maid because her family couldn't afford to keep her anymore. Talk about waking up one day and looking in the mirror only to ask, "How did I get here?"

On February 25, 1967, the biggest blessing in their lives—and without a doubt the biggest blessing in mine—occurred when they arrived in the U.S. As the story from my father goes, "Your uncle had to come pick me up at the airport and sign for me." When my parents arrived here, they instantly had a problem: They had no plan, they knew no process, they had no education, and they had no money. Possibly worst of all, they came here without knowing a word of English. Yet their wholehearted intention was to plug into the American dream.

My father had been a barber in Portugal, which is extremely ironic given that, when I was little, the haircuts he gave me sucked and made me look ridiculous. In fact, as I've gotten older, I've come to recognize that I'm not 100 percent sure he was all that good of a barber in any country! I mean, he cut hair in Portugal back in the '50s through the mid '60s, then switched careers, and the styles here were just...different. In reality, the issue wasn't that he didn't know how to cut hair, it was that he didn't give the haircut that I (or anyone else for that matter) actually wanted. He gave the haircut that *he* wanted, that *he* thought would look good. Even at the car dealership where he worked, he'd cut people's hair after the workday ended, and nobody ever said, "Hey, Lopes, cut it like this..." He just started cutting. You either accepted that or found another barber who would cut your hair the way you wanted *and* do it for free.

You can't be a "real" barber in New Jersey (as a full-time job anyway) if you don't have a license to do so, and it was impossible to pass the test to get your license if you didn't speak English. The necessity to earn money, along with my father's ability to be extremely handy with tools and machines and fix just about anything, landed him a job as a mechanic with a bus company. He worked there for a gentleman named Jerry Curcio. Jerry so loved and respected my father that in 1971, when my parents saved enough money to buy a house but experienced great difficulty getting a mortgage approved due to illiteracy, the language barrier, and their lack of citizenship, Jerry stepped in and co-signed the loan. Then, when Jerry became ill, he closed the bus company. So, in 1975, my dad got a job at D'Amico Lincoln Mercury in East Brunswick, New Jersey, unknowingly paving the way for me to follow behind him and get my start in the automotive industry.

In the thirty-four years he worked there, he never had a proper title. He wasn't ever the General Manager. Or a Sales Manager. He didn't even sell cars. What he did was fix each and every single thing thrown at him, making himself completely indispensable. Any new car that ever came in with a problem, he fixed it. If something broke in the dealership, they would "Go Get Lopes." Toilet wouldn't stop running? Go Get Lopes! Lights in the showroom wouldn't turn on? Go Get Lopes! Alarm went off at 2:27am? Even the alarm company was instructed to "Go Get Lopes!"

My parents stepped it up as best they could, but to be honest, given the way that they grew up in Portugal, just living in America period was a major "step up." In 1986, just fifteen years after purchasing their house, they completely paid off their mortgage. They have otherwise always lived "clean," as my father refers to their lifestyle to this day, meaning that they have *never* had any debt. When you're brought up in an environment as poor as the one they were brought up in and then start to make money, you do one of two things: spend it all right away or live the rest of your life with a bit of a scarcity-based "What if this is all there is?" mindset. They went with the latter approach.

While that was their perspective, I saw life through different people as a young person than they had, and I believed in the possibilities. From an early age, I was exposed to Ed D'Amico and the salespeople who worked in the front of the dealership. I saw that you could wear a suit and tie, work impressive deals while smoking cigarettes and cursing at each other, and then shake hands like best friends. Additionally, these salespeople all drove nice cars, which had me instantly believing that they made good money. Observing the lifestyle of the family my mother was a housekeeper for here in the U.S. also showed me that there was another level beyond ours at which people were living.

My uncle (the one who signed for my parents when they arrived in this country) had come to the U.S. in the late '50s. He started working in restaurant kitchens and moved himself up to the point where he owned his own restaurant. I remember the way he'd walk around with his pants pockets serving as storage compartments for the wads of cash he felt the need to carry around. He drove a big 1973 Imperial LeBaron, and he lived in a huge house. His restaurant was the centerpiece of all the goings-on in town. Everyone knew him and spoke very highly of him.

I also recognized that each of the people in these positions—from the auto dealership to the restaurant—didn't appear to be any smarter than anyone else. In fact, many of them didn't appear to be that smart at all. In my mind, only doctors and lawyers had seemingly unattainable positions because they had to be *extra* smart to get through eight years of college. But these other guys—the guys who sold fancy cars and wore nice suits and crisp white shirts with french cuffs and had wads of cash in their pockets every time I saw them—they didn't have college educations. I don't think most of them even finished high school. There was clearly a whole other way to be able to achieve success and make money than becoming celebrated neurosurgeon Dr. Lopes or Frank J. Lopes, Attorney at Law.

Fast-forward a few years. Ready to graduate from high school, I was working at the auto dealership as a gopher as well as at a local auto parts store as a "whatever." I decided to attend community college, but after the first couple of months, I determined that I just didn't like it, and after the first year, I quit. I don't even remember what I intended to study; that's how inconsequential the whole thing was. All the while, the sales guys at the dealership—you know, the ones wearing the crisp white shirts—recruited me to move to the showroom. So I bought some suits and white shirts, and I sold cars at the dealership where I basically grew up. I learned firsthand what the terms "baptism by fire" and "thrown to the wolves" meant, and it was awesome.

After some time, I stopped selling cars and went to St. John's University, and at the same time, I met my first wife. I quit after a semester, and when I was about twenty, I worked part-time for a liquor distributor as a driver. A few years later, I switched to a job doing the same for a beer distributor. I was also working for a newspaper on Friday and Saturday into the wee hours of the night, delivering bundles of newspapers to convenience stores, gas stations, and other spots where newspapers were sold.

I was living paycheck to paycheck, and the situation was bad. We were raising two kids by that point, and it was a dark time for me. I knew I wasn't where I was supposed to be. I wasn't connected to what I was supposed to be connected to. I wasn't doing what I was supposed to be doing. I wasn't following my dreams or my mission (nor did I know what they were). On April 30, 1994, with the first day of May right around the corner, a completely empty refrigerator, and a looming rent bill, something happened that would change my life forever.

We most often purchased groceries at a store called Shop 'n Bag, which was commonly (and accurately) referred to as "Shop 'n Gag" (sorry, Shop 'n Bag). That Saturday afternoon, the last day of the month, we were walking around the grocery store with only seven dollars to our names, knowing we had to feed our family of four (or, at the very least, our two kids) with it. I thought, "There's no meat that we can buy for seven dollars. What do I feed these two kids if there's no meat?" Then came the idea: SPAM.

My two-year-old son was sitting in the little basket seat at the front of the cart, watching me without having a clue how messed up the situation was at that moment. Meanwhile, my daughter—who was six at the time—was holding onto the side of the cart as I'd taught her to do.

That day, with a can of SPAM in hand and tears in my eyes, and said to myself, "I will never, ever be forced or force these kids to eat anything ever again. What we eat going forward will not be by force, it will be by choice. It will be what we *want* to eat." Even with my strong-willed conviction that day in Shop 'n Gag, I was wrong. Fast-forward exactly seven weeks to Friday, June 17, 1994, which will forever be referred to as my awakening day. (It also happened to be the day of the OJ Simpson "chase," which makes the date easy to remember.)

Let me tell you, you know you're legitimately broke when your tax return makes you feel like you won the lottery, no matter the size of it. When you're like, "Look at all this money! We're in the clear now. It's all good. We've got no more problems!" With a mindset of relief and celebration, we picked up and went to Wildwood, New Jersey and got a room at a place called the Pink Shell Motel (not surprisingly, it's no longer there). Because, of course, what does one do when they are broke and get a $1,000 tax refund check? THEY GO ON VACATION AND SPEND EVERY PENNY!

Everybody wanted to go on a sightseeing cruise to see dolphins and whales, and I had enough money for three of the four of us to go, so I stayed behind. Instead of watching the OJ Simpson chase play out on TV, I sat on the balcony staring at the ocean, silently admitting to myself, "Man, my shit is fucked up." I'd just gotten a $1,000 check, and I was already back to having no money, wondering what in the hell was wrong with me. That was the day when I knew that something had to change, and that something had to be me.

I instinctively knew that the change had to come from within because of the fact that I'd seen others—my uncle, for starters—who were successful by their own choice and pure will. Meanwhile, I was going nowhere but down. Fast. It sucked. Sometimes a movie character has a moment when they recognize that life has to change, and they are the only one who can change it. Believe it or not, that's almost exactly the way it happened for me, because that's the way I'm wired. When I hit a point of no return, which can be represented by the arrival of an opportunity that deeply resonates or just waking up one morning feeling a certain way, it's a reality from which I can't turn away. That day, the reality was that I couldn't go with everybody on the dolphin cruise, knowing that I was, once again, out of money.

I knew that I wasn't going to be able to transform my life by simply dreaming about something different, nor was I going to be able to do it with sheer force. I'd already tried both approaches; neither worked. I needed a process. I needed a plan. I needed to know exactly where I wanted to go and how I was going to get there. Because all I was doing was endlessly drifting. I wondered what I could do to better myself while waiting for the next opportunity to line up, and one thought immediately came to mind: I can read.

I had no money to go to Barnes & Noble, and YouTube was not yet invented. So I took my broke ass to the public library and the dollar bookstore, and I read anything and everything I could get my hands on. First, I read *Swimming with the Sharks* by Harvey Mackay. Even after all the books I've since read, that one book provided me with the greatest and most lasting motivation. After that, I read *Unlimited Power* and later, *Awaken the Giant Within*, both by Tony Robbins. Then I picked up *The Seven Habits of Highly Effective People* by Stephen Covey.

I inhaled the books. Each of them gave me exactly the information they promised to give. I read each, got to the end, and was so pumped up that I felt like nothing could stop me. But then, there was a problem. There was no process to follow. No step-by-step methodology. The books gave me an *idea* of where I wanted to land, but they didn't tell me how to get there. They just said, basically, "Feel this way, and look at your problems like this."

Think about a dog that spends most of his days chained to a tree finally being let off the chain. What does he do? He runs! He takes off with no plan, no destination, and very little awareness. He just starts running, and sooner or later he finds himself either completely lost or run over by a car.

I was like the dog that had just been let off his chain. But I had to stop aimlessly running. I had to come up with my own plan, and in order to do so, I had to take a little knowledge and wisdom from one resource and a little from another. I took something that I'd heard in church one Sunday and combined it with something Harvey Mackay had said and combined that with a tip Tony Robbins gave and put it all together into a methodology that felt like it would work for me. Then, one day, the opportunity to implement everything that I'd learned presented itself.

I saw an ad in the newspaper (while delivering bundles of them at 3:00am) for advertising account executives, and I somehow got the idea in my head that I could do that. I didn't have a resume, so I went to our local Walmart, bought a typewriter, and—if I remember correctly—"borrowed" paper from the library while checking out a book on how to write a resume.

Once the resume was completely typed out, I packed that type-writer up and returned it to Walmart. A typewriter I'd likely never use again was not a luxury I could come close to afford-ing at that time. Thankfully, I got the job as an advertising ac-count executive for the *Asbury Park Press*.

You just never know how one event in your life will seam-lessly blend into another when you least expect it. Back when I was working as a liquor distributor, I had much of North Jersey as part of my route, including some extremely affluent areas in Bergen County. I frequently made deliveries to the exclusive Ridgewood Country Club, and it was always the last stop on my route. In order to make deliveries, I had to pull right up to the front of the club; the place was so old that there was no service entrance. My delivery truck would immediately be in a sea of German luxury and sports cars.

I became very friendly with all the guys who worked in the kitchen and also checked in orders. My delivery was made late enough in the day that I often arrived when they were all eating dinner, and they always included me. We'd eat rice and beans one day, chicken and rice the next, whatever they'd whipped up for themselves. If they weren't yet eating, they'd make me a tuna fish or chicken salad sandwich to eat before I got back on the road.

Once I was working at the *Asbury Park Press*, I was in charge of the automobile dealers featured in the Classified sec-tion. My manager came to me one day and said, "Hey, on Fri-day, we're going to go have lunch with someone." That "some-one" was known to be one of the most successful men in auto-motive advertising in the tri-state area, and his agency placed ads in our newspaper. I asked where we would be going for this lunch, and my manager responded, "Ridgewood Country Club."

When we arrived, the man we were there to meet was seated at a big round table in the corner. He was sitting with his "assistant," his back to the corner, facing everyone in the room. I sat down opposite him, with my back to the room. As I casually turned around to observe the room, I saw Phil Simms, quarterback of the New York Giants, casually eating his lunch, while at another table was legendary New York City news anchor Chuck Scarborough.

As the lunch continued on, I became more and more aggravated. The person with whom we were meeting—this incredibly successful advertising executive—was, if I can be blunt, a jerk who name-dropped more often than the minutes on the clock ticked by (which they did very slowly). Referencing a conversation he had with one of the umpteen bearers of dropped names, he asked the rest of the table, "If you died today, and you went to heaven, and St. Peter said, 'You can go back right now. But you have to go back as somebody else. Who do you want to go back as?', what would your answer be?"

Everyone around the table gave their answers, and none of them were worth remembering. I don't even remember what *my* answer was, but I'll never forget this guy's answer.

He said, "I'd come back as me because I'm having too much fucking fun!" He didn't even answer the question right; the whole point was that you're supposed to come back as someone else.

In that instant, I thumped Bob Sims (no relation to the Giants Quarterback sitting at table number 31) on the leg under the table, said, "I gotta go to the bathroom," and got up. Bob was the classic career "ad guy" and my mentor at the time. While standing at the urinal, I said, "I'm quitting on Monday and opening my own advertising agency."

"What are you talking about, Frankie! Did you hit your head or something?" he asked.

I quickly snapped back. "Do you realize where we are? And who we're with? Did you see Phil Simms over there eating his reuben sandwich?" I asked.

He cluelessly responded, "Phil Simms is here?"

I continued, "If the idiot who we came here to see—the 'I'd come back as myself' asshat—can get to this level, I can get to a level that none of us can even dream of. And I'm not going to waste any more time in my life just talking about this."

The following Monday, I quit.

I figured that it would be a good idea to work for somebody who had an agency first in order to learn the basic framework. But, long story short, that play went a bit awry. Even though I'd given my notice to quit and on Monday morning I was supposed to start at the agency, I went right back to the newspaper offices as though I never quit. I told my boss the real story behind what had transpired and committed to staying at the newspaper for "a little while longer." By the grace of God and my boss's kindness, he allowed me to do so.

A month or two later, I again left the newspaper (this time for good) and started working for an agency with employees I eventually became partners with and then quickly bought out. By 1998, I was officially running my own advertising agency.

Seven years after my 1994 awakening day, I was finally running a thriving business. In fact, I owned and operated one of the largest as well as the top-ranked advertising agencies in New Jersey, a state loaded with them. *NJBiz,* New Jersey's leading business journal, listed out the fastest growing companies, and ours was in the Top 50 in the state. Our clients were some of the area's largest and most successful automobile dealerships, retailers, and up-and-coming businesses, including

Gary Vaynerchuk's family wine store, Wine Library (yes, *the* Gary Vaynerchuk). I was thirty-two years old, and my income was eleven times higher than it had been seven years prior. I thought I had life and business mastered.

In 2006 or 2007, there was a small Italian restaurant operating in New Jersey near our home. We used to go there to eat three or more times per week. We'd become friends with the chef, who was also the owner, and one night he told me that even though the place was always busy, he was losing money hand over fist and was probably going to have to shut down sooner rather than later. He was a really nice guy, so I loaned him one month's rent for the restaurant to help keep him afloat.

I said to him, "Pay the rent, and just don't charge me to eat." He then proposed the idea that I purchase the restaurant. I could barely order a meal properly, much less run a restaurant, but my ex-wife really wanted to buy it. I sensed that she had no idea what running a restaurant actually involved, but she believed otherwise. So we bought it. That was probably the biggest mistake of my life. (The second biggest mistake was buying the second restaurant. Standby for that story.)

Within a year of purchasing the first restaurant, my agency was running on fumes. I could see that the car business was not going to recover any time soon, and I knew I needed to do something to keep us from going under. There was another restaurant in downtown Freehold that had been dramatically successful for a long time, and the owner suddenly needed to sell it due to some personal issues. I was able to purchase it for next to nothing, so I figured I might as well get into it and see how it went. The first one was still doing exceptionally well, so it seemed reasonable to get into this new one, given that I knew the agency was going to fold before long.

Both restaurants continued to be busy for a time as I worked to keep the agency above water. I kept trying to explain to my then-wife that owning a restaurant isn't a job; it's a lifestyle…a culture. You don't just show up and greet people on Friday and Saturday nights while celebrating a flood of cash into your bank account. It was incredibly intense and tiring work. She ultimately recognized that. But, by the time I knew we were really in trouble, I was spending 100 percent of my time during the week trying to keep every automobile dealership from committing suicide and engaged as a client of the agency while the restaurants were running. It was absolutely ludicrous.

And then, I lost everything. And I mean *everything*. I had to sell or shut down all three of my businesses—the advertising agency that I'd started from scratch and the two restaurants as well. The agency failed for two big reasons: the economy imploded, and I took my eye off the ball. The car business at that time was in a terrible slump, and the majority of our clients were car dealerships.

Let's just whip through the details of the next few years. My marriage fell apart. We got divorced. I got remarried. That ended up in another divorce (that's two marriages and divorces, for anyone who's counting). And, lo and behold, I found myself in August 2011 with no house, no car, no money, no vision for the future, no nothing. I was sleeping on a couch. Not my own couch, mind you. Not my parents' couch. My daughter's couch. My own kid was in a better position in life than I was at that time. But every good comeback story starts with sleeping on someone else's couch, right? I remember waking up one morning, shuffling into the bathroom, exhaustedly looking into the mirror, and asking, "How did I get here?"

I was able to scrape together (translation: borrow from my parents) enough money to rent an apartment—an apartment that never should have been rented to me given that I had no job and no income. But I *knew* that I could do more. I knew I could again earn the kind of money I'd previously earned. I knew that I wasn't defined by where I was. The biggest difference in my perspective was, while I wanted more and knew that I could do more, I was also clear that I wanted a *different kind* of "more." I wanted someone to hug me the way Adrian hugged Rocky. I wanted more special moments—more of those moments that, when they're over, you look back on and think, "Dammit, that's over, and I hope something like that happens to me again."

The money, the cars, the fancy houses, the polished shoes and watches, all that is great, and I'm not putting any of it down. I like a $75 steak just as much as any other guy. But, if you don't have the other stuff—the relationships, the moments, the meaningful connections, the Adrian and Rocky hugs, a brain that's consistently in the right place—do the fancy things really mean anything? Is it cool to have a big house and be sitting in it alone? Is it fun to have pockets stuffed with cash but nobody to share it with? Is it exciting to have an expensive car but nowhere to go? The money, car, and house are all byproducts of implementing a process that works. They aren't the means *to* the process, nor are they the direct result of it. They're the byproducts.

Interestingly, almost as soon as I started to work on further honing my methodology, my past started to creep up, unbeknownst to everyone around me. Everybody (including my friend and former client, Gary Vaynerchuk) was like, "Frank, man, it's great to see that you're back! What you went through was hard." I tried to divert from these conversations as quickly as I could because I was carrying around all the shame and the pain and the anxiety of the past. I woke up every single morning and took all that pain put it in a bag, flipped it over my shoulder, and headed out for the day. Mind you, everything in that bag was made-up.

This is part of my personal life mission: Get each and every person who is walking around carrying a bag of their own pain to stop carrying it around and simply put it down. If you're carrying around a bag of self-inflicted anxiety and pain, I'm giving you permission right now to put it down. There is so much strength and power that comes from *not* carrying it around any longer. The reality is that nobody cares about your pain. Nobody cares about your anxiety. So please, don't even load up the bag in the morning. There is nothing to be gained from doing so.

I have fully embraced the belief that I have to teach as many other people as I can what I did to arrive in this place, because if it worked for me, it can and will work for you. I'm not that smart. If I can make it work, *you can make it work*...and probably much better than I did.

My definition of "having everything" may not match *your* definition of "having everything," and that's just fine. And, if it all falls apart again based on something entirely outside my control, I have the confidence of any GOAT doing their thing that I can, by employing The 7-Minute Setup method, get myself right back to whatever measure of success and greatness is right for me at that time.

The 7-Minute Setup works by keeping you hyper-focused. The minute you lose your focus, you start to drift. And when you start to drift, what happens? You spend an hour watching cat videos on YouTube, that's what happens.

The entire system is based on realistic time frames. A lot of the goal setting methods out there just don't work because the time we're encouraged to set aside to reach a goal is simply too short. Or too long. The timeline has to be realistic in today's environment in order to allow you to keep evolving, because as you're going through life, other stuff is going to come in that you can't control and to which you'll have to react. You can't simply skim through The 7-Minute Setup and then unconsciously run with it. You have to be able to *evolve* with it; you have to be able to adjust. What's fascinating is that, over time, it seemingly evolves with you.

One thing I want to be super clear about is, you have to do this for you. You can't be doing it while saying, "I want to do this for my family." You've got to do it for yourself, first and foremost. I've always said that "taking care of yourself is the most selfish thing you can do for everybody else," and I stand by that wholeheartedly.

Consider for a moment the age-old question "How do you eat an elephant?" and its answer: "One bite at a time." Each daily 7-minute setup represents one intentional bite of that elephant.

Your overall 7-year vision, which is where we'll get started, is made up of seven key focus areas in which you need to get powerfully clear in terms of the way you want your life to look seven years from now. You've surely heard of all of them and likely considered most. But allow me to present them in a way that may have been a bit foreign until now. Get comfortable, and prepare to set yourself up for the growth, prosperity, fulfillment, and happiness you've always dreamed of.

1

7-Year Vision

Your 7-Year Vision revolves around seven promises that you will make to yourself in seven specific areas:

- Home
- Finances
- Health
- Relationships
- Control of time
- Spiritual
- Career/impact

You'll start at a macro level in each area, and then break out the top-level details into specifics as microscopic as you wish. As you'll see, each of these areas feeds into one other—or multiple other—areas. They are all intimately linked in one way or another, so if you're misaligned in one area, it's going to affect another, and so on. Maintaining balance between the areas over time is critical to staying on track with the vision you're working toward.

Given that each focus area bleeds into the others, creating a massive spider-web-like phenomenon, you can fall into that web as though it were a giant, comfy, strong hammock and happily swing in the breeze. Or, you can suddenly find yourself with a disgusting, sticky spider web all over yourself, causing you to flail around while losing your mind. What's important to note is that both webs are built in exactly the same way. The question is, which one are you consciously or unconsciously building? Because you're always building one of them.

Building the spider web that is super sticky and gets stuck to your face and has dead bugs in it is a lot easier than building the extremely comfortable hammock-like web. While the choices required to build the icky one come with far less resistance, in order to build the comfy hammock, you'll have to make hard choices. You may have to decide to sell your current home and downsize. Or refuse to continue to zone out by watching cat videos at work. You may have to commit to getting out of bed at 6:00am and going to the gym (if a healthy body and mind is part of your vision, and 6:00am is the only time in your day when you can exercise). You may have to commit to not eating a half gallon of ice cream every single night.

You have to be self-aware enough to know what you want, and have the self-discipline required to execute a plan that will get you there (which is precisely what this book will teach you how to do).

What do you want your life to look like seven years from today in each of the seven key focus areas? Don't think about ten years from today; ten years is too long. When it comes to your overall big vision, seven is the new ten. When I start to think of myself ten years in the future, the first number of my age is six. I don't want to think about that. If I do, I'll stop and put the whole thing away. But, if you want me to talk about who I can see myself being at fifty-seven years old? I can see that. I know what I want to be and have at that point. Identifying that is an easy task, and you'll notice that to be true at any age.

Your 7-year vision is the vision that clarifies the promises you're making to yourself when it comes to the "big stuff." For example, perhaps you want to own an automobile dealership or be a real estate developer. Or, you want to start a family, Or, you want to have a family already established (and maybe it's still growing). Or, you want to live in a big house by the ocean. (Every single person who has employed this method wants to "live in a big house by the ocean," by the way. Every single one.)

**In order to get clear about what you want,
you have to acknowledge what you don't yet have.**

A bit of forewarning: Going through this exercise may be painful, and more so for some people than others. It will be painful because, in order to write down what you want, you'll have to actually acknowledge what you don't yet have. You'll have to acknowledge what you're missing. You'll have to really feel it—the "not having" of it. I have watched people genuinely weep while writing out this list in front of me, and through that process, I've learned that I can no longer have anybody write this list in front of me, because when they start to cry, I start to cry!

Your list may include some (or all) of the following:
- I live in a house overlooking the ocean.
- I'm a successful personal trainer.
- I own my own business.

- I am the #1 salesperson in my company.
- I'm in the best physical shape of my life.
- I am financially stable and have paid off all debt.
- I have a strong relationship with God (or the Universe, or Buddha, or whatever spiritual power you most resonate with).
- I am in a deeply satisfying romantic relationship.
- I am surrounded by deep, loyal friendships with people who bring out the best in me.

It just so happened to take me seven years to accomplish some of my bigger goals. I was able to accomplish a few in a bit less than seven years, and there were a couple that ended up taking a bit longer than seven years. But when I say a little less or a little more, I'm talking about only a couple of months. The time required to reach the goal wasn't dramatically longer or shorter. And, when I started looking into that more thoroughly, I identified the long-standing divinity of the number seven, which historically plays a mysteriously common role in both religion and culture.

The number seven is featured in the titles of a number of bestselling books, including *The 7 Habits of Highly Effective People* by Stephen Covey, *Seven Years in Tibet* by Heinrich Harrer, and *The House of Seven Gables* by Nathanial Hawthorne. It's the total number of wonders of the world. Repeated three times (777), it represents the biggest payout on a slot machine.

It also has significance in nearly every major religion. There are seven days in the week (in the Christian faith, it is said that God rested on the seventh day), and the Book of Revelation speaks of seven churches, seven angels, seven seals, seven trumpets, and seven stars.

The Koran speaks of seven heavens. Muslim pilgrims walk around Islam's most sacred site seven times. Hinduism has seven higher worlds and seven underworlds. The Buddha took seven steps after he rose. Maya, the birth mother of Siddhartha Gautama (the Buddha) is said to have died of joy seven days after giving birth to him.

In Hindu weddings, the bride and groom walk around the holy fire seven times during the ceremony. A priest reads mantras as they do so. After they have each completed this ritual alone, they take seven steps together and say a vow for each of the seven steps.

Many legends and mythological stories are associated with the number seven. Zeus took pity on the seven sisters and transformed them into stars. The number seven is the sacred number of Apollo (the son of Zeus).

An article on PsychologyToday.com notes:

"In 1956, George Miller of Harvard University wrote what is today considered one of the classic papers in psychology in which he demonstrated that most people can retain roughly seven items of information in their short-term memory. That is why phone numbers in the U.S. and many other countries tend to have seven digits (area code notwithstanding)—as it is the most digits most people are likely to recall (although cell phones have done away with the need to recall anyone's phone number, even our own)."

Mathematician Alex Bellos, author of *Alex Through the Looking Glass: How Life Reflects Numbers and Numbers Reflect Life*, asked 44,000 people to state their favorite number, and the vast majority of them replied with the number seven.

There are seven colors of the rainbow, seven notes on the diatonic scale, and seven letters in the roman numeral system.

Snow White hung out with seven dwarfs. There are seven continents. The optimum number of hours of sleep for human beings is seven.

On a lighter note, perhaps you witnessed (or participated in) the then-somewhat-popular Seven Minutes in Heaven game as a younger person, or have declared yourself to be in Seventh Heaven, even though you didn't necessarily realize what that phrase meant beyond "I'm very, very happy." Because we've been, perhaps subconsciously, "groomed" to be comfortable with the number seven, people are quick to easily accept the idea of a 7-year vision.

I want to take a moment to clarify the fact that these focus areas are listed in no particular order. The fact that the first area is Home does not imply that Home is the most important or critical area. Frankly, you could start with whichever of the seven you'd like, and you'll find that, at some point, they will still intersect, which is why they are each critical. If you want to run a ten-figure-a-year business, you may also determine that Home is a hotel, your relationships consist of Siri and Alexa, and your health is driven by high cortisol levels (or you might decide that you'll have an on-the-road trainer, whom, I suppose, you could also count as one of your primary relationships). If that feels good to you, it's perfectly fine! It may not feel good to most people who recognize that the ten-figure-a-year business and overflowing bank accounts don't leave much room for that relationship they desire or the control of time that allows them to travel as they'd like to. Therefore, they modify the ten-figure-a-year business goal to an eight-figure-a-year goal. That, or they live their own version of "upscale mediocre," wherein they have a lot of "stuff" but are miserable. The goal is to avoid that reality just as much as it is to avoid settling for a mediocre life simply because you believe that's all that's available to you.

Home

The first area in which you're going to establish your 7-year vision is Home. The Home focus area allows you to get clear on a variety of factors, not the least of which is the actual location of your primary dwelling (unless your vision is not to have a primary dwelling at all, and instead spend your life switching locations every three months, which some people decide to do!). *Is where I'm living convenient to the rest of my life?* is the biggest question to ask in order to kick off this focus area is. *Is it convenient in terms of where I work, where those important to me live, its affordability, the stores and retail establishments I frequent, and the places I enjoy visiting for entertainment?*

When thinking about where geographically you live (or want to live in seven years' time), consider what you want to feel on your skin when you walk outside each day. Do you want to feel warmth? Do you want it to be cool? Do you want the temperatures you feel to change with the seasons, along with the type of clothing covering your body?

What do you smell? What do you see when you first wake up in the morning? What do you see when you get in your car and drive around? Asking these questions will help you clarify your ideal vision. If you want to feel the warmth on your face, do you want to feel that warmth every day or only once in a while? If you want to feel it every day, that likely indicates that you want to live in a warm place. So, if you presently live in Michigan, that means you'd need to move to Florida, Arizona, California, or Texas.

Is where you're living right now conducive to your health? It's one thing to live in Michigan; it's something else to live in Arizona; and it's yet something else to live in Florida. I've known many people who have moved from, say, the East coast to Arizona or Tennessee or Texas and declared that they'd never go back for one reason or another. Once they see what it's like to live somewhere else, they can't imagine returning to the place where they've spent the majority of their life or the past several decades.

On the flip side, there are people who wind up moving away and then coming *back* to the place where they grew up. Bruce Springsteen is a great example. He grew up in Freehold, New Jersey and always thought he wanted to leave the area the first chance he got. Most of the songs he wrote early in his career touched upon that. And he did. He's lived in a number of different places and traveled all over the world multiple times. And his primary residence is now ten minutes away from the house he grew up in. He realized that he wanted to be in New Jersey, so he moved to an area one town east from the one he grew up in, which happens to be about ten minutes away from my home.

Where you live has a tremendous influence on your balance and prosperity. You have to be in the right environment in which to thrive. If I lived in New York City, my head would explode from the craziness of it. If I lived in a super small town, my head would explode from being so far away from everything!

Beyond the state and city in which you live now (as well as the one you'll promise yourself to live in seven years from now), what kind of house do you want? We all truly *need* little more than a two-bedroom condo. But what kind of home do you *want* in order to be most content? Is it a one-story house?

A two-story condo? Do you want the master bedroom on the ground floor so you don't have to go up and down stairs any more often than necessary? How many square feet do you need? Do you want a large backyard with rose bushes and a grassy lawn? What details make it so that you can thrive?

Whether more weight is given to the geographical area or the structure in which one lives depends on the person. Today, I wouldn't be comfortable living in a condominium. Unless it had a beautiful water view; that might change things (There's that "house by the ocean" concept again!) Someone might be living in the house of her dreams, but if it's situated in the middle of no-man's-land South Dakota, she might not thrive terribly well there.

There are people who say, "I want to live in Beverly Hills," so they move there, but they live on the very outskirts, like the ghetto, of Beverly Hills (does that exist?) just so they can say they live in Beverly Hills. And they're miserable because the cost of living is so high, and they aren't having the experience they thought living in Beverly Hills would provide. Or, they lease a Mercedes so they can say they drive a Mercedes, but the payment makes it so that they can't afford to pay for the gas it needs to run. When all is said and done, they're living in Beverly Hills or driving that Benz simply to alleviate some sort of insecurity.

Your specific living arrangement is also an important factor. For example, you could be living in your own apartment right now, and while you might really enjoy living on your own, the cost of doing so is making it so that you can't do other things that you'd like to be doing, like starting your own business or traveling once or twice a year.

Maybe you're sixty-two years old, and you love having a roommate because you don't like living by yourself. But, if you decide you want to live in Redford Falls, Montana, finding a roommate is going to be difficult because there are only about seven people living in that town, and the likelihood that one of those seven wants to live with a sixty-two-year-old is probably pretty small.

Perhaps you've recently graduated from college or are otherwise new to the workforce, and you have a roommate with whom you can split costs. And maybe that roommate is an absolute slob. Also, a jerk. They come and go at all hours and make all kinds of noise. They never give you their half of the rent on time, nor do they help keep the apartment clean. So, you're getting half the bills covered, but you're living in an extremely stressful situation that's not working for you.

Perhaps you are a parent and your adult child or children are living with you. Or, today you have four kids under your roof, but in seven years you'll be an empty nester.

It's important to think through how you're living now, what's working for you and what isn't, what your life will look like in seven years, and how you believe you'll want to live at that point in order to get the maximum amount of joy from life, as sustained by your home.

As I mentioned earlier, each focus area blends into another or others. Home nearly always starts to blend into the second focus area, Finances, at some point. Part of your vision may be that your home is paid off. Part of your vision may be that you have a roommate to help you with costs. Part of your vision may be that you don't *need* a roommate to help you cover costs!

If you desire to live in a 3,500 square foot house in the suburbs, you're going to need to make a certain amount of money to be able to afford that lifestyle. If you have the conviction that you're going to live in NYC in a 3,500-square-foot apartment on the Upper West Side, it's going to run you an ungodly amount each month in rent. If you buy it, you're looking at a one- to God-only-knows-how-many-millions-of-dollars purchase price, and you'll therefore need to earn at least a million dollars a year to be able to comfortably pay that mortgage.

So when it comes to the area of Home, when thinking about your life seven years from now, what resonates as a ten for you (on a scale from one to ten)? Regardless of what you might believe is possible sitting wherever you are right now, what do you most *desire* for your life to look like when it comes to the geographical region and actual structure you call home?

Get out a piece of paper and give yourself twenty or so minutes to work on a rough draft of this. You can hone it (or expand upon it) over time. Remember, this is an ever-evolving process. Start each declaration with "I have…" or "I am…" As I'll clarify in a bit, the way you phrase the components of your 7-year vision is critical. For now, simply start with simple statements such as "I live in a six-bedroom home in Monmouth County, New Jersey" or "I share a beautiful condo in Florida with my partner and two kids" or "I am so excited to walk outside each morning and tend to my backyard garden, even in the middle of January, without getting frostbite."

When you're ready, we'll hop into the next focus area: Finances.

Finances

I could easily sum up the category of finances by simply saying, "If your money ain't right, you ain't right."

As mentioned previously, the city and dwelling you desire to live in may require that you pay a $7,000 monthly rent or an

$11,000 monthly mortgage payment. But the opposite could be true as well. Perhaps the place you dream of living is actually less expensive than your present payment, or perhaps you're planning to downsize within seven years (which would likely make this lower payment—or no payment at all—possible). It's important to have a sense of what it will cost you each month to live in the home you choose.

Part of your finances also includes your debt. Maybe you're currently living in a 7,000-square-foot house in the suburbs and have a $9,000 mortgage payment, but you're only bringing home $12,000 a month and eating SPAM every night (have I mentioned that I hate SPAM?). If this were the case, your 7-year vision may include downsizing your house in order to up-size your financial position.

Maybe you're nearing retirement age, and you can't upsize your finances anymore (or simply don't want to). You're going to have to shed the $1,000 per month lease on the Lexus your significant other drives. You're going to have to shed the $6,000 mortgage payment. You're going to have to shed the $1,500 custom suits you buy every month. Those are just a few examples of the ways your living situation can and will affect your finances or the way that, if you're not making enough money because you're not working to your potential, it'll screw up your overall living situation.

In seven years' time, will you have debt? Will you still be paying off college loans for yourself or your kids? Are you able to dine out as often as you'd like—and at the restaurants you most enjoy going to—without fear of your credit card getting declined? Do you vacation once or twice a year? When you do, where do you go? Are you a Ritz-Carlton type of guy, or is the campsite your thing? How much money do you have stored or invested? How much do you want available to you at a moment's notice?

To get right down to it, when you look at all of the items that end up on your 7-year vision, which of them will require money? I will encourage you to break down each and every piece of your vision and reverse engineer it. My own 7-year vision includes financial promises to myself such as:

- "My annual income exceeds ten million dollars."
- "I will generate at least $100,000 per year in speaking fees."
- "Our house is paid for in full."
- "I have over $1,100,000 cash in storage."

It's important to put a dollar figure on each of your visions in each category, whenever possible. If you say, "I have enough money in the bank to feel comfortable," how much money *is* that for you? For some people, perhaps $100,000 would be enough to live out their remaining years quite comfortably. For others, one million dollars might be nowhere near enough. If you don't have a target, it's nearly impossible to come up with a plan to meet it.

Just to quickly touch the surface of the third focus area, Health, and the ways in which finances affect that area, consider that anytime you begin to absorb increased financial stress, your health starts to become affected. You'll wind up with a tremendous amount of cortisol in your body, you won't be eating right or exercising, and you won't be getting good sleep. All of this will affect your performance at work, which will affect the amount of money that you'll make, which will affect your finances, which will give you more stress.

For those of you who might think, "Bring on *all* the money. As long as there's a ton of money, I'll be perfectly fine and stress free," imagine that you're Carmela Soprano, living in a beautiful house in North Jersey. (If you didn't watch "The Sopranos," don't worry; you'll understand this reference in seven seconds.) You essentially have unlimited cash and all the free time in the world. You can go to the gym any time you want, and you have the money to buy expensive food, hire a chef, and buy all the high-end gym attire your heart desires. But your husband is Tony Soprano, he's sleeping with a Russian whore, and you're miserable and want a divorce.

Don't end up that way. The way to make sure that you don't is to identify the financial goals you promise yourself to meet within the next seven years.

So now it's time to go back to that piece of paper (which is likely going to become several pieces of paper over the course of this) and begin to detail your 7-year vision in the area of Finances. Again, start with "I will…" and "I have…" statements, and we will hone them from there once we get through the remaining five focus areas. Also, whatever costs you come up with, add ten percent. You've heard about inflation, right?

Health

Do you want to die?

That question truly encapsulates this focus area. If the answer is yes, you can put down the book, because nothing that I'm going to say from this point forward will matter.

Still here? Fantastic! Next question: Do you want to live your life from this point forward in the best state of health that you possibly can? To more effectively help you answer that question, I'd like to put a few visions in your brain. Vision Number One: Have you ever had a friend or family member who suffered from some type of health ailment? If so, do you remember the pain and stress that it put them through? Do you want that kind of pain or stress in your life?

If you answered any of those questions with "no"—you haven't had a family member or friend who suffered with an ailment—think of a TV show or movie in which somebody fell ill. Do you want to be in that type of position one day? Obviously, we're all going to die. Death is the undefeated heavyweight champion in the game of life; it gets everyone eventually. But, even knowing that to be true, do you want to travel down the road that is your life with the least amount of stress and pain so that you'll hopefully simply die peacefully in your sleep one day? Or, do you want to make it so that you have a long, anguishing end, spending months in the hospital or otherwise being cared for by someone else?

Our health is constantly evolving as we get older. There are always going to be new challenges. My state of health ten years ago was different from what it is today, and it's going to be different ten years in the future.

Listen, I'm banking and praying that by the time I reach my mid-seventies there are going to be cures for Dementia and Alzheimers, because my mother currently has them. But I'm also hedging my bets that there's *not* going to be a cure by then. I'm not just going to sit back and say, "Oh, by then they'll figure that out." I'm doing everything I can today to reduce the risk that I'll get it, knowing that I may have the gene and that, therefore, falling prey to that wicked beast is inevitable. But, even if that is true, I want to do everything I can to ensure that it doesn't happen, or that I can delay its onset and severity for as long as possible.

Making promises and setting goals for your physical health is essential, but setting goals for your emotional and mental health is also critically important. Health, at the 10,000-foot level, refers to the level of health that can be seen (physical) as well as the level that can't (mental and emotional).

Perhaps you know that you and the bottle of Tito's vodka are too good of friends right now, and based on your latest set of bloodwork results, your doctor is heavily encouraging you to consume less alcohol. In that case, one of your health-related visions might involve drinking alcohol less often, if not becoming completely sober. Maybe, if you've already gotten sober, your vision includes staying that way.

That's really it. Do you want to die? And when you do (because we all will), do you want it to be painful, not only to you but also to all of the people around you? Unless you want to die earlier and with more pain than necessary, commit to always being in the best possible health that you can be.

You know what time it is! Get out that journal, notebook, or stack of paper you've been documenting your vision on and begin noting the promises you make to yourself in the area of health. Examples (just to jog your creativity) include:

- "I am in the best physical shape of my life."
- "I consume NO processed foods."
- "I work out at least 6X a week."
- "I fall asleep every night with ease and wake up each morning with energy and enthusiasm."
- "I am off all of my diabetes and blood pressure medications."
- "I am less anxious than I have ever been."
- "I feel confident and comfortable with exactly who I am."

Relationships

Let's talk about relationships and the way that they tie into the other focus areas. As with each of the other areas, there are a lot of different angles from which to look at relationships. Number one, there's your relationship with your self (the word "yourself" is purposefully split into two in this instance). Please do not discount this relationship, as it's truly critical to all other relationships. After all,

If *you* don't know who you are, who the hell is everyone else getting to know and build a relationship with?

Next, there's your relationship with your significant other. That relationship will do one of two things: add to your life or take away from it. Those are the only two options. It's very cut and dried. When most people are asked for the first time into which camp their relationship falls, their answer will more than likely be a lie. To be blunt, if it takes you longer than .01 seconds to answer the question, you're in trouble. The answer to this should be an absolute no-brainer. Of course that doesn't mean that there aren't tricky moments and even longer-lasting challenging times. Every relationship has its ups and downs. But if you don't know straight out of the gate whether or not your relationship enhances your life or detracts from it, it's the latter.

Beyond your relationships with yourself and your significant other, you have relationships with family members, and that includes your children. Most everyone says they do what they do "for their kids," as though the kids will be kids forever. The fact of the matter is that those kids are still people. They have their own agendas, and there will come a day when they will be grown-ups (believe it or not) with their own daily challenges to contend with. Some of those challenges will involve or affect you, while others will be addressed behind completely closed doors.

I'm about to make what may be an unpopular statement, but here goes: While you may instinctively see your kids as part of your daily or weekly life—even once they're grown and on their own—they don't owe you any type of relationship just because you're their parent. You can't assume that they're going to show up every Sunday for dinner (at least not willingly) if that's not the relationship that you've built with them over time. If that sort of dynamic is important to you, one of the items in the relationship category of your 7-year vision needs to relate to consciously and intentionally building the kind of relationship that makes your kids *want* to come over for dinner on Sunday nights and not sit at the table looking pissed off and wondering when they can go home already.

When you have a child, you are instantly given the responsibility to raise him or her. You don't get a medal for doing that. You don't get bonus points for doing it well during one particularly chaotic February, and you don't get negative points for making honest mistakes. What you "get" is no more complicated than the daily choice not to be a jerk so that you don't have to take responsibility later on for having raised a jerk who's drifting his way through society.

The reason that our kids don't owe us anything is that we're just doing what we are supposed to do—there's not really any "above and beyond" involved in that, and you see that most clearly with parents who have children with severe emotional, mental, or physical challenges. While society understandably sometimes wants to give those parents a medal for going above and beyond, their response is most often a confused, "This is my child. Of course I'm doing all of this. It's the hand I was dealt and the risk everyone takes when having a child."

You can derive the same amount of guilt or pleasure, frustration or happiness, from any family member, immediate or extended. The result of this is that sometimes, people build the type of relationship with family members whereby those people don't want to see them every Sunday, every other Thursday, or even on major holidays. If the relationship has a bad foundation and you therefore have a bad long-term relationship that's never resolved, it could adversely affect your mental and emotional health (which can affect your physical health). Never underestimate the power that guilt over the choices you've made has in affecting your health in one way or another.

For the majority of my life, all of my extended family has been absent. Growing up, it was mostly my mother, my father, and myself. I had two uncles who came to the states, but one went back to Portugal and the other passed away in the late '80s. With my father being the second youngest of thirteen and my mother the middle child of eight, the Lopes family is not lacking for members. Those people, however, are all in Portugal. They have absolutely no relationship with me, and I have none with them. Many people have suggested, "You should go there and meet them." Novel idea, but…um…what would I say to them? "Hi, I'm your cousin, Frank. Do you guys have McDonald's here?" After the initial hellos and discussions about Cristiano Ronaldo, the conversation would be pretty much finished.

Because I've never been a part of a large family, large family gatherings have a tendency to freak me out. I am more comfortable speaking to 1,000 people I don't know than I am sitting down with a dozen relatives. As I write this, we're coming up on the Thanksgiving holiday. The running joke for the last two days has revolved around the painful pride people have around the fact that they're hosting forty-seven people for dinner, six of whom they can't even remotely tolerate, and they have to leave work early because they have thirty-four pounds of potatoes to peel. They won't see these forty-seven people again until the following Thanksgiving, when they'll all descend upon the same doorstep to pretend they care about what's been going on with everyone for the past eleven months and gossip about Aunt Betty, who's again drunk and napping in the corner. This is just my observation from attending other families' Thanksgiving dinners.

Now, having forty-seven people in my house who I *choose*, who are my family, even if not by blood? That sounds more fun. But people often don't nurture certain relationships and then still expect that everyone will get together on significant holidays when they wouldn't get together on a random Thursday in May.

Beyond immediate and extended family, you have your crew (which we'll talk about in great detail in just a bit).

Then, there are the people with whom you're forced to associate every single day. This includes the jackass you run into every morning who works the drive-thru at Dunkin' Donuts, Starbucks, Tim Hortons (or whatever coffee place you frequent). It includes the receptionist where you work—whom you walk by and say hello to on your way to your office even though she snarls without so much as looking up each time. It includes your customers, your clients, or your patients. It includes the other doctors in the practice, the other brokers on the floor, or the other realtors in the office. It includes the idiot at the gym—you know, the guy who always slams down the weights because he insists on making sure that everybody else knows how heavy he's lifting. You're having a relationship with all of these people in one way or another. Sometimes, the relationship lasts for only a quarter of a second per day, but that quarter of a second may feel so miserable that it makes you stop wanting to go to the gym.

Side note: I left a gym once because of an asshat like that. Just a year later, the same asshat followed me to the new gym. *FML*.

Let's say you're a realtor who loves to help people buy and flip houses. But, when you get a client you don't get along well with, you suddenly decide that you hate your job. The thing is, you don't hate your job; you dislike that particular client. You don't need to quit your job; you need to quit that client and be more selective about who you work with going forward. Perhaps have coffee with prospective clients first to make sure your personalities are complementary.

There are other jobs where you don't have as much control over who you're working with. Let's take the automotive industry, for example. In most cases, salespeople are expected to serve or sell to anyone and everyone who comes through the door. The customer may be degrading or downright rude, but the expectation is that the salesperson will serve them with a smile. There may come a time when that salesperson believes that he simply cannot deal with one more annoying customer. But he still has to go in there every day and wonder, each time those front doors open, if the person coming in is a jerk or not, and that fact makes him feel depressed. That depression leads to a health decline and makes it so that instead of just getting past that person and earning a commission, the salesperson isn't bringing his best self to the situation. He starts to blow deals, which winds up affecting his finances, and then he ends up getting fired, and his relationship with his significant other becomes extremely strained because his financial situation is uncertain.

If your relationship with your significant other were one wherein you could call him or her and simply say, "Listen to this!" and laugh about it together, that might make the situation more tolerable in the short term while you're looking for something else. But, if your spouse is calling you every hour on the hour, pestering you with, "Did you sell any cars yet today?" things can go downhill in multiple critical areas in a hurry.

I know what it feels like to have a client who's simply not a good fit, and with whom I absolutely dread meeting, even over the phone for just thirty seconds. In the particular instance to which I'm referring, I knew from the start that it was a bad fit. I took on the account because it was a referral from a friend, and I therefore didn't follow my gut. When we took on the account, the client's business was struggling, and his day-to-day disposition of course reflected that.

Sometimes when I take on a new client, their store is running okay, but they've had a falling out with their old agency or weren't working with any one agency consistently and instead were using nine different vendors to manage their marketing (their sales strategy was something they just "kinda make up" as they went along). Or, the store's a complete mess *and* they were using nine different vendors. One way or another, there's always a transition of some sort, and for one reason or another, the client is usually a bit stressed out. That part I'm used to. They're stressed out, but they're optimistic. That was the biggest red flag with this client—he wasn't optimistic; he was impatient. I reminded him that the turnaround was going to take time. There's no magic pill, no silver bullet. But he wanted a magic pill, a silver bullet, a gun that hit the bullseye every time, even without aiming it. Success comes via a combination of different things, and it takes more than a week to figure out what that correct combination is for each particular client. We start with the marketing part, then move to lead handling, then move to the sales process. Each piece of the process has to be handled methodically and with patience. By the end of the month, the dynamic and daily conversations had gotten ridiculous, so the relationship was respectfully severed, and I reminded myself how important it is to trust my initial feeling about a new prospect, regardless of whether or not he or she was referred by a friend.

All of my contracts with every one of my clients run "month-to-month," meaning they can be cancelled at any time. I want to have just as much power and the right to fire the client as the client has to fire me. When I start to dread going to see a client for a regular meeting, I know that I have a decision to make: check out and let them pull the plug, or be straightforward and say, "If the relationship is going to continue this way, I have a few numbers I can suggest that you call instead of mine, because this dynamic is not working for me." As is also the case with personal relationships, there are times when professional relationships are simply no longer a good fit.

If you're a business owner, and you have an employee who is dragging everyone down, you have to be willing to quickly fire that person—even if you hired him or her with great expectations. I understand that you might feel compelled to help them grow into the best version of themselves, but ultimately, if growing into the best version of themselves isn't their choice, it's insane to believe that you can get them there through willpower alone. Sooner or later, they will be the cancer that kills the morale of your entire staff.

While perhaps a bit dramatic, cancer really is the best analogy for this scenario. Think of it this way: If you had cancer in your kidney, would you spend time lamenting the fact that "If the doctor takes it out, I'll only have one kidney left!" Would you meditate and send the cancerous kidney good energy, hoping to make it feel more at home? I highly doubt it. Perhaps you'd have to admit that you were improperly angry at the cancer, given that you were the one who produced it through all the bad food you ate combined with the years of smoking and alcohol you consumed. But, while you're busy worrying about what it might be like to have only one kidney and being mad at the one that "betrayed" you, the cancer has spread to the *other* kidney. Now what? Now you're in real trouble, that's what.

Now that we've covered four of the seven focus areas, I have to take a moment to ask, how much longer are you *still* determined to wait to look in the mirror?

Because the longer you stall and sit in this limbo of "Maybe it'll get better, maybe it will change," the more the other areas of your life are degrading. The hole you're digging is only getting deeper and deeper.

Take ten or so minutes to think through the relationships you have in your life today. Which do you promise to nurture? Which do you promise to let go? What's most and least important to you when it comes to your relationships? When you consider what your life looks like in seven years, what is the best possible outcome in terms of the relationships you have in your life?

Control of Time

In short, every single human being needs to own that they are—in the long run—able to be in nearly complete control of how they spend their time. If that weren't true, indentured servitude would still be a thing. Having control over how you spend your time is absolutely essential, not just for thriving and living a happy life but also for having a life that you're not outright miserable living!

The minute we feel a sense of "Oh my God, I'm out of control," it's a bad sign. We use that phrase and others like it to bring attention to things that aren't going well, telling someone to "get a grip" or admitting, "*I've* got to get a grip." How many times in your life have you felt that you were doing things you were forced to do, either by yourself or by somebody else? Perhaps you were forced by your own fears, or perhaps you were forced by your own feelings of not being good enough (which is, essentially, a form of fear). Whenever you have that feeling, it won't be long before everything goes bad. Think about this the next time you suggest to yourself or someone else that things are "out of control." Pay attention to the way so many important areas of your life (or your perception of them, at least) seem to quickly crumble under this notion.

My father's a good example of this concept. He talks about how much he hates living in America (he's been here for fifty-three years, mind you), but the reason he says this is that he romanticizes life back in Portugal. He thinks, *If I lived in Portugal, with money and a more mature outlook, I could live like a king.* The reality is that he also realizes that the exact same stuff he gets frustrated by here in the U.S. is there too—in fact, it's worse there. But what he romanticizes is a life living in northern Portugal where he could see Spain on the other side of the bridge, on acres and acres of grape vines, with chickens and donkeys running around the yard. In that vision, the sun comes up every day and there are no problems to contend with. That's what he remembers from his own childhood. But (and it's a significant but), he leaves out all the years of being poor and the struggle that went along with that.

Since they arrived in America, my mother (who, remember, was forced to leave home to be a chambermaid for a family in Lisbon at the age of eight because her parents couldn't afford to continue raising her) had been dying to come here. Doing so was her idea, because you could come to America and both be and do anything you wanted. These days, she unfortunately doesn't know what town she's in, much less what country, but if we rewind a little bit to a time when her brain was 100 percent healthy, she would be adamant about never returning to Portugal. She used to ask my father all the time, "Are you crazy?" when he'd speak of returning. She'd say, "It's the same over there as it is here, except we *know* all those people! Here, we can stay under the radar. No one wants anything from us except taxes!"

Those opposing ends of their life rope pulled at each other for years. But, my dad is also the guy who will remind you that if you have even the smallest bit of talent coupled with a ton of will, you can be ultra-successful in this country precisely because you can make money doing all sorts of things. You can make money digging holes in the ground; you can make money sweeping a floor; you can make money cleaning a toilet. So, as long as you have a tiny bit of talent (and everyone does in one area or another) and a good bit of drive, your chances of being successful here are one thousand times higher than they are anywhere else in the world. He'll be the first to remind those of us born and raised here that we take that for granted.

Think about the times when you felt like you didn't have control over what was going on around you and stop saying you "have to" do something. In most cases, you don't *have* to do *anything*! People say, "I have to go to work today." No, you don't. You could sit at home on your ass and watch "Sponge-Bob"; it's on all day long!

Anytime you say, "I have to (fill in the blank) today," it should be an immediate clue that something's off.

It means that whatever fills in that blank is messed up. That you really don't want to do it; you're forcing yourself to for whatever reason. Why is that? Are you forcing yourself because you need the money? (See how we just went back to Finances?) Do you need the money to pay the mortgage? (See how we just went back to Home?) We say, "I have to go to the doctor" when we ate horribly our whole lives, and now we're in trouble. That's when you can legitimately say you "have to" do something. But nobody ever says, "I have to go on a vacation to Bali" as though they're dreading it.

The phrase "I have to" is so ingrained in us that we don't even realize what we're really saying most of the time. We heard our parents say it, we heard our grandparents say it, we hear people on TV say it. And I'm just as guilty of this as anyone else; I have to check myself often.

If you don't have control of what you're doing and not doing, of what you want to do and don't want to do, of what you look at every day and don't look at every day, that's something for *you* to make an intentional effort to change—even if you do so gradually. People say, "If you love what you do, you'll never work a day in your life," and while I understand what they're saying, the fact is that there's a timeline to that. You might say,

"While I love my primary job, I sure hate doing my own accounting, but right now, this is what I'm choosing to do because I'm not yet in a position to hire it out." And then, you promise yourself that you'll hire an accountant within the next seven months.

Spiritual

The Spiritual focus area is always an interesting topic of discussion. Many people will say that they need to be connected to some kind of higher power. Others will say, "When you die, you die. The lights go out and that's the end." But still, that's a belief. The Spiritual and Control of Time focus areas are intimately related in the sense that you have to be in control of what you believe, and you have to be able to believe what you want to believe, the way you want to believe it.

People have to have a foundational spiritual belief, even if that belief is that they're an atheist. You cannot live like Spock with zero emotion unless you're a sociopath. At a bare minimum, you must own that you're an atheist who wants to have the most fun that you can while you're here. You're not going to live forever. This isn't *Interview with a Vampire*. Speaking of which, did anyone ever stop to consider the possibility that vampires may hate the fact that they live forever? Like, maybe they're miserable that they're 764 years old!

Bottom line: You need to be in contact with whatever it is that drives you spiritually and practice it. Further (but just as important), don't look down on someone else for not practicing the same belief.

Career/Impact

Your career—or the way in which you make an impact—first and foremost connects to control of your time. There is a difference between career and impact, and both are important. Sometimes they overlap more so than others, but one's career absolutely affects his or her impact, because, if properly leveraged, that career can greatly increase one's impact.

Maybe you have a job you hate. You're great at it, but you hate it. Perhaps you feel most alive when you sing or play the piano. If that's the case, you need to find a way to scratch that itch, even if it's not (yet) through whatever you're doing full-time. I also believe that everybody on the face of the earth wants to make sure that, in one way or another, whether big or small, their life meant something. Because there comes a day in everyone's life—for some it comes sooner, for others it comes later—where they realize that they are just a cog in a magnificently colossal wheel. In the five minutes before you leave this life and move onto whatever you believe comes next, you want to know unequivocally that, during your time here, you actually did something. The thought of those five minutes is what drives me more than anything else. I don't want to get to the point where I can't do anything about it.

There's an episode in "The Sopranos" during which Carmela goes to Paris. She's standing in the middle of the ruins of the Roman Baths, looking around, and she thinks, *This city is so old.* You think of all the people who have lived there—generation after generation, for hundreds and hundreds of years. All those lives. Damn, it's so sad; in the end, it just gets washed away. In those moments, you can quickly realize that one day you'll be gone, that the clock is always ticking, that the expiration date of the time you have to make an impact here is written *inside* your body, where you can't see it, and it's always changing to sooner or later based on the choices you make each and every day. The question is, what do you want to be known for? What type of impact do you want to make?

Let's say you want the opportunity to be the Pope who is remembered for taking the Catholic Church in a new direction, the way Pope John Paul made so many changes to the church that he is now a saint and referred to as "The Great."

Let's be absurd (it's fun) and suppose that I promise myself that in seven years I will be the Pope. If I'm the Pope for only long enough to consume three cups of coffee before I keel over, I will have been a Pope, but I won't have made any degree of real impact, so it's important to recognize that while my career would include being the Pope, my impact would be determined by how I chose to use that time. As the Pope, perhaps my promises to myself would include making it so that women could become priests and priests could get married, for starters.

But, before I spent too long simply dreaming about becoming the Pope, I'd have to create a 7-year vision that supported that desire. Fear not—the purpose and execution of the 7-year vision is coming to you in the next chapter. First, I'd have to become Catholic (if I weren't already, which I am). Then I'd have to attend seminary in order to become a priest. After becoming a priest, I'd need to become a bishop. Then, a cardinal. Then, the current Pope would have to die. At which point, the Conclave of Cardinals would convene to nominate candidates for the next Pope. I'd have to be nominated and then receive the most votes (and I'm sure I missed a step or two here).

Once I'd received the most votes, the career would be determined, but the impact would still be up to me. While I was working to become Pope, my intention for impact would be one thing (as represented by my 7-year vision at that point), and after I became Pope, my intention would likely shift (as would my 7-year vision).

But there's nothing that says that you have to become Pope to make this sort of sweeping impact. Perhaps one has a spiritually based goal of becoming as influential as Joel Osteen or Benjamin Netanyahu.

What do you promise yourself that you are going to pursue in order to make an impact on the planet? On another life? On a community? Is your career aligned with that? (It's okay if it isn't; identifying that your career and your impact provide different solutions to different problems is a monumental step in the right direction!)

Before we continue, it's critical to make seven promises to yourself in the seven focus areas. Some of you will have a simple macro promise such as, "I promise I am living in a three-bedroom house in Austin, Texas," while others will break that macro promise down into the intricate details of what your home's exterior looks like, what variety of wood cabinetry is installed in the kitchen, how tall your baseboards are, and the scent of candle sitting next to your bed. There's no right or wrong, and truthfully, the more detailed you can get the better, because as you start to put details to the dream, you'll only get more and more excited about making it a reality.

Address each focus area and promise yourself what your life will look like in each one seven years from now. You can use the space on one page to detail your promises, or you can get several pieces of paper and detail them there. You'll want to keep these promises somewhere convenient so you can refer to them often. Therefore, I don't recommend writing it in a journal that will sit closed. You can, however, replicate it into your journal if you'd like in order to refer to it each morning or evening and have something incredible to refer back to seven years from now (or even seven months from now) when you'll undoubtedly be well on your way to making those promises a reality!

Now that you've made yourself some important promises in the seven key focus areas, it's time to determine how you will bring those promises to fruition. This is where The 7-Minute Setup method takes center stage and, step by step, week by week, month by month, gets you to a life you could, until now, only dream about.

The first thing that people do when they find out that they're going to visualize what their life will look like in seven years is add seven to their current age. I recently began working with a twenty-three-year-old at my gym named Dylan. The first time I saw him, he was wearing a Grant Cardone 10X baseball cap. I thought, "I have a few of those 10X hats, but they're the earlier ones." More notable was the fact that Grant had signed them. I was pretty sure I had three in my closet.

I approached him and said, "You're all about Cardone and shit, huh?"

He replied, "Yeah, totally." I told him that I had some of the hats from when they first came out, that they were signed by Cardone, and that I'd be happy to bring him one the next day. I went home and looked through all the hats I had, and as it turned out, I had one that was signed plus a few others that weren't signed but were made from a Dri-FIT material—the kind you'd wear to the gym—so I threw them into my truck to take to him.

He had told me that whatever time I planned to go to the gym the next day would determine what time he went. We met up in the weight area, and I gave him the signed hat as well as the one for use at the gym. I didn't tell him that it was my last one; I just said, "You can wear this one when you workout so you don't screw up the one that's signed." From there, we continued to chat.

As it turned out, he'd looked me up on Facebook after we met the day before. He asked, "What's this 7-Minute Setup thing?" and in response, I asked him, "Do you want to do it? If you do, I'll coach you through it."

When we started with his 7-year vision, he immediately said, "Okay, by the time I'm thirty..." and I immediately stopped and redirected him: "No, in seven years." The point is that no matter your age when you start, it's going to take approximately seven years to accomplish the biggest goals you'll set forth. You could be fifty, and you'd think to yourself, "Seven years from now, I'll be fifty-seven." However, fifty-seven itself means nothing. It's a number. That's it. So, I discourage people from using age as a point of reference. Additionally, I *encourage* people to think in terms of seven years in the future because their 7-year vision is going to be refreshed within those seven years, likely more than once. The list isn't cast in stone. It evolves over time. As you'll learn in Step Two, you're going to reevaluate the 7-year vision every seven months.

Dylan, who is in pharmaceutical sales, initially said that he hated his job, didn't feel fulfilled in it, and knew that he would include a greater sense of personal happiness (as well as a career change) in his 7-year vision.

Fast-forward just a few days, and he let me know that, through writing out his 7-year vision, he realized that he in fact *didn't* want to quit his job. The job he's in has a lot of restrictions and guidelines that must be followed. He feels like a dog on a leash much of the time, whereas he'd rather run free and do what he needs to do. That conflict initially made him think he wanted a new job entirely. He also wrote as part of his 7-year vision "I own a Lamborghini Diablo."

"Dylan, you could drive that Lamborghini Diablo down the street and get hit by a friggin' bus and smash that thing up," I told him. "But, if you work on *yourself*, the result of that can never be taken away." That resonated with him. I then reminded him that all that stuff—the material stuff—is simply a byproduct of one's goals; it's not the goals themselves.

After taking a hard look at what he was doing, how much he was earning compared to others his age, and what the potential was in that career path, he went from believing "I can't do this job; it's too restrictive" to taking a more powerful stance by acknowledging, "These are the rules. And I'm going to accept them because it will allow me to accomplish my 7-year vision." Going through the 7-year vision exercise empowered him to be able to see what his goals and options really were, and once he saw them written down, he was in a more powerful state of mind because he recognized that he wasn't working within a predefined box. He was instead working within a set of guidelines. He realized that there are going to be guidelines in place, no matter what, for the rest of his life. He also recognized that if he left the job he was in, he'd quite possibly only be trading one headache for another. Sure, he might get another position with fewer restrictions, but maybe he'd hate the people he'd be working with or the hours would suck, or the position would be far less lucrative financially.

He concluded that what he's doing is actually *right* for him at this point in time—it's providing him with a steady income, experience, and stability, which is what he really needs and wants. He's more interested in pursuing his spiritual growth and learning about himself, because he knows that if he continues on the road that he's on without being connected to himself, his likelihood of failure is going to go up exponentially. Plus, if he's able to set aside some of his income (he's paid very well), he'll be able to take more chances later on when he has more knowledge, skill, and experience.

Of course, your life is going to change during the course of these next seven years. Unexpected events are going to occur. In addition, your life is connected to the lives of other people who have their own agendas and their own long- and short-term goals. And, as those people go through their lives and their agendas, it can affect yours and cause you to alter your goals. For example, my wife might put on her 7-year vision that she wants to live in a big, beautiful house by the ocean. Then, through the course of living our lives over the next year (or three), we might determine that we need to be in Arizona. There's no ocean in Arizona. You have to maintain the flexibility necessary to change your list based on what it is that you've already accomplished as well as other people's agendas and the way the natural path of your life unfolds.

You may put something on your list today because it sounds like a great idea, and then, as you start to get closer to it, you find yourself thinking, "This sucks. I don't want this. Do you mean to tell me that in order for me to achieve this, all of this other garbage comes along with it? I have no interest in doing that whatsoever." So, you take the overall goal off of your list. Or, you adjust it because you've learned over the first year, two years, or five years, that you really don't want what you thought you wanted in exactly the way you thought you wanted it. The adjustments absolutely represent success; they show that you're becoming clearer about what you *do* want and where you're going. The list is a living, thriving organism that you continue to nurture.

Dylan's initial 7-year vision included goals such as:

- I have a beautiful home in Alpine (a ritzy area in New Jersey—along the Hudson River, of course).
- I have a beautiful, strong, compassionate, faithful, independent, hard-working and ambitious wife.
- I have two beautiful kids.
- I have retired both of my parents.
- I have a matte orange and black Lamborghini.
- I have matte black Rolls Royce.
- I have donated $250,000 to charity.
- I have $5 million invested in the stock market.
- I have $5 million in liquid cash.
- I have four real estate investment properties.
- I have two Rolex watches.
- I have bought my mom, dad, and brother their dream cars.
- I have complete control of my mental health and well-being.
- I have gotten myself into my best physical shape and condition.
- I have established a strong relationship with God.
- I have established a strong public speaking and motivational business coaching company.

The instructions I gave him before he got started were the same instructions I give to everyone: sit down and think about what you want your life to look like seven years from today. Consider *every single aspect* of your life. What do you want to hear? Do you want to hear little kids playing? Do you want to hear the pitter-patter of little kids' feet in your house? If the answer is yes and you're my age, that likely means that you want to have grandchildren. If you're twenty-three or twenty-seven years old, it probably means you want to have kids of your own.

When someone says, "I want to have $5 million in the bank," I remind them that it's not going to come to them for free. They're going to have to earn money in order to accomplish that goal. A lot of people say they want to be debt-free (which is what the statement "I want to have $5 million in the bank" often represents or is related to). But getting there requires that you make enough money to be able to pay off your debts *while maintaining your lifestyle.*

One task I give people right away is, take all material possessions off of your list, with the exception of the possessions necessary for life, such as a dwelling. But the fancy car, the fancy watch, the boat, and the Birkin bag are all byproducts of having money in the bank. That's all stuff that comes once you make more money and can truly appreciate having it in your life. That's when you cherish those items a lot more; they actually have extra value attached to them because you're already deeply fulfilled in your own life. But, at the same time, *you're* not attached to them. You don't depend on them as a means of validating your worth or your accomplishments.

Years ago, I had all that material stuff, and the truth is that it was all there merely to fill holes, to replace stuff that I knew wasn't right in my life in the area of relationships, work, my self-confidence, and the way I felt day-to-day in my own skin. I thought, "If I get this Rolex, I'll feel better" or "If I get this Mercedes, I'll feel better." That kind of thinking never ends. It becomes its own drug. I was filling my body with the high that comes from buying a $30,000 Rolex—but once the dopamine wore off, I was left with a Rolex and far less money in my bank account.

And, I still hated myself.

So what was the actual point of buying the watch? If I'm in a place where I love myself, and I buy a watch I genuinely love, it works, because I'm not attached to the watch in order to continue to love or value myself. I'm instead in a place where I love myself no matter what, and that makes me love and appreciate the watch even more.

Dylan's original vision included living in a house in Alpine, which is in North Jersey.

I asked, "Why do you want to live in Alpine? Is it because half of the New York Yankees and Chris Rock and Eddie Murphy live there? Or because you like it?"

He replied, "I've never actually been there before."

Including that goal as part of his vision was based solely on the fact that Alpine is an area where wealthy people live. I informed him that, for him, Alpine might suck, at which point he looked at me like I'd just given him a matte black Mercedes. Once he threw out that goal, we were able to confirm that he wants to live closer to where he lives now, and he altered his vision of having a beautiful home in Alpine to having one in Red Bank or Rumson, New Jersey (also nice areas).

With regard to his goal of buying his parents their dream cars, I asked, "How dare you? Who are you to say what your parents' dream is? Maybe they want their house paid off or want to move to Florida! You have to ask them what *they* want!"

People who are closer in age to me (in their fifties) tend to want completely different things than the younger set wants. They want financial security; they want their credit card debt to be paid off; they want their children's debt (such as college loans) to be paid off; they want their homes paid off. They want to have the flexibility and freedom to do whatever the hell they want to do at any given time. They're more concerned about their health, physical appearance, and physical well-being.

There are no goals that are off-limits in this initial goal-setting session (even though we ultimately remove those that fall into the materialistic category). I've had several clients say, "I want to make my parents proud of me." And then they tell me that both of their parents have been gone for years. Some people are still trying to accomplish goals that they don't believe they've yet accomplished. They also tend to have goals related to whatever form of spirituality they practice. This is likely because they're trying to hedge their bets; none of us knows what's coming next. I believe it's very smart to hedge one's bets in this way because, if you think about it, anything that goes along with any positivity-based religion or faith is good. "Thou shalt steal from thy neighbor" is not, to the best of my knowledge, a commandment of any faith. Neither is "Thou shalt be jealous of everyone and talk about them." Religious and spiritual principles are, at their core, good. So why not hedge your bets and have some spiritually based goals, because with them in place, you'll wind up living a better life.

Or, I'll hear that someone wants to go after new dreams; perhaps they want to become a chef or share nutrition tips or help underprivileged kids learn about physical fitness because if—when they were younger—they had known and practiced what they know now, they'd be in much better shape instead of being in a position where half of their body is breaking down and they're spending at least four days a month in the doctor's office.

There are no limits to this stage of the process because it's important that you purge all of your goals out of you without judgment or overthinking. As I mentioned earlier, people who do this exercise in front of me often start crying. When I ask why they are upset, they say, "I can't believe that I have all these things that I want, and I have none of them" or "I have so many things that I want to do, and I've done none of them." The self-reflection and subsequent shame begin to kick in, and it takes people on a bit of an emotional journey. And that's okay; in fact, it's better than okay. Because the best way to build something solid is to completely tear down the old structure and build from the ground up, even if that means moving some heavy rocks that might just not want to be moved.

The 7-year vision exercise takes some people five minutes to complete, and it takes others hours. If it takes longer than a day, it's an indicator that you're just putting it off because you don't want to admit that you're missing a whole hell of a bunch of things in your life that you want to have.

The second step of this part of the process (after you've listed out all of the high-level details of your 7-year vision and removed any purely materialistic goals) is to identify the items on your list that are connected to one another and can, therefore, be accomplished simultaneously. For example, you can group items that pertain to your overall health. If you want to have a particular physical appearance, that appearance is perhaps tied to losing weight, eating healthier, and having a fitness routine. Your big house by the ocean is connected to your income. Grouping goals in this way will make it less overwhelming when you get to the next step and break your 7-year vision into your 7-month waypoint goals.

Let's say one component of your 7-year vision is, "I have lost weight and am healthier and more physically fit than I've ever been." If, in order to accomplish that, you set a 7-month waypoint goal of going to the gym five days per week, that goal will take you closer to losing weight, having a physical appearance you are happier with, *and* being healthier overall. In this way, one step can help you accomplish three of your 7-year visions at the same time. A new, more lucrative job will help you reach your income goals *and* your goal of being debt-free. Taking just one step can move the needle for several elements of your 7-year vision.

Next, you have to write the final list, and you *must* write it by hand (your own) on paper. In a Forbes.com article, Mark Murphy, author of *Hiring for Attitude*, notes that "vividly describing your goals in written form is strongly associated with goal success, and people who very vividly describe or picture their goals are anywhere from 1.2 to 1.4 times more likely to successfully accomplish their goals than people who don't."

Understanding why an act is so impactful often helps encourage one to take it on. Continues Murphy, "Writing things down happens on two levels: external storage and encoding. External storage is easy to explain: you're storing the information contained in your goal in a location (e.g., a piece of paper) that is very easy to access and review at any time. You could post that paper in your office, on your refrigerator, etc. It doesn't take a neuroscientist to know you will remember something much better if you're staring at a visual cue every single day."

In addition, he notes, encoding is occurring. "Encoding is the biological process by which the things we perceive travel to our brain's hippocampus where they're analyzed. From there, decisions are made about what gets stored in our long-term memory and, in turn, what gets discarded. Writing improves that encoding process."

When you write your list, do so in accordance with the five Ps: Pure, Perfect, Positive, Possessive, and Possible.

Pure

Your goals have to be pure, meaning that your intentions when it comes to each goal must be pure. Your goals can't be predicated on bad or malicious intent. The goal cannot be "I'm finally going to get my mother-in-law back, that bitch." That is not a goal that belongs on the list, because it's anger-filled. Instead, perhaps the goal is, "I am enjoying wonderful and fulfilling relationships with every member of my family."

Perfect

When I say perfect, I mean that nothing in the world could screw it up. It's perfect by your standards and your standards alone. It's perfect for you. In no way shape or form should there be any reason in your mind as to why you haven't reached this goal within seven years. You write down the goal with the certainty that everything that needed to fall in line did...that all the stars aligned in order for you to reach this goal.

Possessive

Possessive implies that it's happening right now. The vision is written as "I have $1 million in the bank," not "I will have $1 million in the bank." Another example is "I have a wonderful, loving spouse," not "I will have a wonderful, loving spouse."

Positive

Hopefully this is relatively self-explanatory. Again, none of the 7-year visions should be related to revenge, anger, or negativity.

Possible

This is a fun one. Yes, I do believe that everything is possible. Almost. I'm fifty years old, so if I declare that, in seven years, I want to be the starting center for the LA Lakers, that's not a possible goal, and I think that Lebron James would support me on that. Similarly, while I could say that I want to be a unicorn for Halloween next year, I can't write on my 7-year vision "I am an *actual* unicorn day-in and day-out." I also can't include "I have grown a sixth finger. Or a third arm." You have to be real when it comes to the vision. To stretch is one thing; to set yourself up for disappointment from the start is another. You want to be president of the United States, but you've never held a position in office and you're already sixty-seven years old? No. Be real enough to say, "I want to be involved in national politics." If you were to start today at a local level, in seven years you'd perhaps have a shot at being involved in politics at a national level.

Again, no material possessions are to be part of your final 7-year vision beyond those required to live. You can have "I live in a beautiful four-bedroom home in Alpine, New Jersey" on the vision, but not "I have a closet full of Air Jordans" or "I have six jet-skis in the garage." Instead, think of material desires in the sense that they are *byproducts* of the overall vision.

When I talked to Dylan about his initial no-holds-barred, complete brain-dump 7-year vision, I reminded him that in seven years, he may no longer want a matte orange and black Lamborghini. Maybe he'll want a really nice Mercedes. Or a Chevy Tahoe. Or, maybe he'll want to have every single penny he's earned invested and making money for him. The point is that the money itself will be there, and he can do with it what he wants at that point. Without reaching *that* goal (money in the bank), the desired byproducts are irrelevant.

Once you get your list written out and fine-tune it as directed above, group your visions into categories and expand upon them in terms of the strategies by which you will reach each goal. For example, if one of your 7-year visions in the health category includes "I weigh 195 pounds, which represents a twenty-pound overall weight loss," you might decide that you need to exercise, eat properly, and make sure you get enough sleep each night. In order to accomplish those goals, you'll go to the gym five times per week, hire a nutritionist, and take the TV out of the bedroom.

By this point, you're likely feeling excited because it's becoming clearer how you can reverse engineer the big goals into smaller, more manageable steps that you can begin taking *today*!

At this point, I must give you another warning so that, when it happens, you'll just acknowledge that it's happening and move forward instead of being paralyzed by it. Soon enough, you'll have a moment when the adrenaline will start to wear off, and you'll wonder, *How the hell am I going to do any—let alone all—of this?* In Dylan's case, he wanted to have five million dollars in the bank, five million dollars invested in real estate, and five million dollars invested in the stock market. So, within seven years, he needed to have fifteen million dollars go through his hands...after taxes! That's a lot of money. I'm not saying that it can't be done, but I am saying that you have to tread the line between "everything is possible" and "this goal is certifiably insane." The way you do that is by ensuring that your vision is actually a possibility.

If you set the goal way too high, in six to eight months you're going to say to yourself, "How in the world am I going to acquire fifteen million dollars in seven years?" You don't have to take time out to have the pity party of a lifetime and then reduce the goal; what you have to do is set the goal up properly to begin with! It goes back to the unfortunate fact that I, Frank J. Lopes, am not going to play center forward for the Lakers. I'm not going to suddenly become a quarterback for the Dallas Cowboys. Dak Prescott, you're safe...for now.

Once you write out (by hand) your 7-year vision, you must put it somewhere you can see it often. l used to tape both my 7-year vision and my 7-month waypoint list (which we'll be talking about in the next chapter) onto the glass front of a framed set of thirty-two one-dollar bills.

This framed collection of random dollar bills used to hang in Ed D'Amico's office at D'Amico Lincoln Mercury—this is the dealership that Mr. D'Amico owned and the one at which my father worked for thirty-four years. It's where I started going when I was eleven years old on days when I didn't have school. My parents didn't know what to do with me on those days. I was too young to stay home alone (and they were rightfully concerned about what I'd do unattended in the house). My mom was a housekeeper, and I couldn't go with her to the houses she cleaned for the same reason. The five words that changed the direction of my life were spoken one morning by my father: "I'll take him with me." The experience of being at the dealership with my father matured me at an incredible rate, and when I was eighteen, shortly after my high school graduation, I started selling cars there.

Ed D'Amico passed away suddenly in the summer of 2001, and his wife, Patty, took over the dealership. By this point, the dealership was a client of mine (I owned my dealership-focused marketing and advertising agency at that time). They were actually the second client that hired me, and that was only because the day I went into business, I first stopped at another dealership while on my way there.

One day, I went into the dealership and Eddie's wife had the framed dollar bills on her on her desk, face down, and she had a pair of scissors in her hand. I walked in and said, "Patty, what the fuck are you doing?" She said she was remodeling the office and was going to cut the dollars apart to get the money out of it. I reached into my pocket as fast as I could to give her thirty-two dollars.

She said, "You want it that bad? Take it!"

I replied, "Patty, I've been looking at that since I was eleven years old."

I picked it up and literally ran through the shop toward the front door. I wanted to get that frame into my car as soon as possible. My father was still working at the dealership at that time, and I remember him calling after me, "Where are you going with D'Amico's money?"

This framed collection of thirty-two one-dollar bills is one of the few things that has stayed with me throughout my adult life. I've always made sure that it was somewhere I could see it daily. It hung in my office at my old agency, and then it somehow made its way to my home office. For me, it serves as a vision board of sorts.

While we're on the subject of vision boards, I want to make a point about this often-recommended visualization tool that might make your head blow off of your body. If you have a vision board, you need to frame it, and you need to put it behind glass. Otherwise, the vision board simply becomes part of the room's scenery. The effect isn't as strong as it is when you put it behind glass and frame it. Doing so makes it come alive. I recommend that you make a copy of your 7-year vision and your 7-month waypoint goals and tape them to your vision board (which, again, I recommend that you have behind glass). What happens is that, subliminally, in order to get to what's *behind* the glass you have to get through what's in *front* of it, which is the 7-year waypoint goals that lead to the accomplishment of the 7-year vision.

If you look closely, the glass in front of the framed dollar bills that hangs behind my office desk is covered with little pieces of clear tape. I'm lazy, so I just tear the visions and goals off when it's time to replace them and whatever tape stays there is left there. I still look at it every single day. It's full of beautiful memories and adorned with the tape remnants of my 7-year visions and 7-month waypoints.

The Importance of a "F**k-It" List

Many people have a vision board. Most people have a bucket list. Many of the items on someone's bucket list will, at some point, make it onto their 7-year vision. In addition to having a bucket list, I have—and strongly believe in having—a "f**k-it" list. This is where you list out things that, should you die having *not* accomplished, who cares.

My "f**k-it" list includes the following:

- Skydiving

- Eating at Red Lobster (no disrespect to Red Lobster—I've just never felt like I need to eat endless shrimp for $11.99)
- Visiting China—it's dramatically overcrowded, and nearly every virus seems to start there.
- Breaking a bone—I've never done it and I'm okay with that.
- Playing rugby—I've never had a desire, plus not playing it keeps me from having a broken bone.
- Having major surgery
- Reaching the final five minutes of my life and recognizing that I didn't make the impact I could have made.
- Snorkeling, scuba diving, or being in the deep end of the pool.

The last items may necessitate a bit of explanation because it's one that people truly don't understand when they first hear it. Who wouldn't want to go snorkeling in a beautiful location? This guy, that's who. I'm okay in the water as long as I can touch the bottom of the pool. As soon as I can't touch the bottom, I lose my mind—like, horribly—because I almost drowned when I was eight years old.

We were on the beach in Atlantic City, shortly before all the casinos went up. It was the first time I'd ever been there, and there was a massive pipe that opened up at the shoreline. When I say massive, I mean eight or so feet wide. With an opening at the shoreline, it ran underwater, sucking ocean water in on one end and pumping it out somewhere else—conceivably somewhere in the city. There was a sign next to the pipe that said "Danger." My mother said to me, in her Portuguese accent, "Frank, be careful over there. That sign says *dannger* on it."

Because of her accent, the "a" in danger was short instead of long. I replied, "Mom, it doesn't say *dannger*, it says *danger*."

Mr. Hooked on Phonics then proceeded to get sucked into the pipe.

I was screwing around in the water, and somehow the suction inside the pipe just pulled me in. I was holding onto the side (my entire body inside the pipe, feet first), little by little pulling myself back to the entrance. My father saw this going on and jumped on top of the pipe. He reached in, grabbed me by my wrist, and pulled me out, the cement pipe scraping the hell out of my chest and neck in the process.

Since then, I won't go into a body of water if I can't stand on the bottom with my head and neck above water. God forbid if you're next to me when I realize I can no longer touch. I will grab you and use you to catapult myself toward shallower water. I will literally push you under the water, put my feet on top of you, and push off. It's horrible.

Another item now on my "f**k-it" list is skiing. I went a couple of times when I was younger, but at this point, in my mind, skiing equals Sonny Bono, which equals dead. I'm out. Now, you may say, "But Frank, you drive your car every day and could get into an accident," which I understand. But the reward of driving the car is worth the risk to me. The reward for skiing or snowboarding? Not worth the risk.

But I won't hold the rest of my family hostage to my refusal to put on skis. We'll find the best place that exists, and I'll happily drive everyone there. I'll pay for everything. I'll get everyone all set up, and then I will find the most comfortable spot in the lodge to sit. When everyone is finished skiing, snowboarding, or otherwise getting from the top of the mountain to the bottom, there will be hot chocolate or whatever else they want sitting there waiting. We will then get back in the car and go home.

Also, in case you're wondering, since that day in Atlantic City, I've never again corrected my mother's pronunciation. That whole experience affected me so deeply that item number fourteen on my "f**k-it" list is "correct my mother's pronunciation."

Most people get tripped up when it comes to one aspect of the 7-year vision, and that is that they don't properly plan to have the money to finance that vision. Let's take the example of having a house by the ocean. You can either pay cash for it, or you can mortgage it. If you pay cash for it, you're going to need to come up with, say, a million dollars in cash within seven years. If you're going to finance it, you need two things: the down payment and the consistent cash flow to pay the monthly mortgage payment. Even if you pay cash for it, you still need the continual income to be able to pay the monthly bills, the homeowners association fees, and the property taxes. Whether the money is coming in from your day-to-day job, dividends earned from investments, payout from a trust fund, or somewhere else, you have to have a plan in terms of where it's coming from.

What most people do is decide what their 7-year vision looks like, identify how much money they will need to finance it, and then immediately throw their hands in the air and think, "My vision is too big." Your vision isn't too big. The issue is whether or not you're willing to do what you have to do to make that vision become reality.

That's a critical distinction: Is your vision too big? Or are you willing to admit that you don't want to do what's necessary to make it a reality? If you aren't, that's okay. It doesn't mean that you're a loser. It means that you're aware of what you are and aren't willing to do. But knowing that, you won't any longer envy or be resentful of someone else who *is* living that vision, because you'll remember that you had the opportunity to choose whether or not you wanted to have that life, and you chose not to. It's a level of self-awareness and ownership that people need to take, myself included.

Once you write out your 7-year vision, feel free to share it with people close to you. Honestly, if any of those people suggests that you're not smart enough to accomplish any part of it that, or declares that any part of it is otherwise not possible, or questions why you would *want* some aspect of it, immediately make a mental note that they're not part of your crew (which we'll talk about in more detail in chapter 7).

So now you have your 7-year vision. You know what you're going after, and you're going to be flexible enough to modify or outright remove anything that, as your self-awareness increases, you realize actually isn't something you want to have in your life. It's totally fine if somebody *else* wants it; it's just not right for you.

Seven years doesn't pass in the blink of an eye. And yet, it does. So the next task is to reverse engineer which goals you can aim for over the next seven months in pursuit of your 7-year vision.

2

7-Month Waypoint Goals

O nce your 7-year vision is established, it's time to create your 7-month waypoint goals. This is the part of the process where you figure out what you need to do over the next seven months—not the next year, the next *seven months*—to inch your way toward your 7-year vision. Just as seven is the new ten when it comes to your overall vision, seven is the new twelve when it comes to your yearly plan.

I call these intermediate goals "waypoints" because they act as mile markers on your journey. For example, when you drive from your house to the grocery store, you know that, along the way, there are certain markers that you're going to pass, such as a corner gas station, neighborhood, or street sign. These are waypoints. If you start driving and don't see these waypoints, it will be clear that you're going in a different direction that you initially intended. The waypoints all lead toward your destination or, in this case, your 7-year vision.

In less than a year, I've watched people accomplish as many

as five of the goals on their 7-year vision. In order to accomplish any one of them, however, you must reverse engineer what you need to do to hit it. Some of the goals may very well have the same waypoint goals—at least up until a certain point. As an example, if I were into bodybuilding and wanted to become Mr. Olympia (and I don't, to be completely clear), I would first have to win a specific qualifying competition. Before that, I'd need to win a lower-ranked competition. Before that, I'd need to sign up for a competition. Before that, I'd need to train for a competition. Before that, I'd need to get myself in proper physical condition to be able to train for a competition. Before that, I'd have to join a gym. Also, I'd have to start eating properly.

Once you've reverse engineered the process in this way, you'd say, "Within seven months, I am..." or "Within seven months, I have..." and then fill in the blanks with actions that are perfect, positive, possessive, pure, and possible.

As you can likely already imagine, this exercise also presents some people with the feeling of "This isn't actually possible because the math doesn't work." As an example, let's say you're a soccer player, and you want to play in the World Cup. Within seven years, there will only be a maximum of two World Cup events, because the World Cup only occurs once every four years. Same goes for the Olympics. Maybe you want to be an Olympic gymnast, and within the next seven years, you'll get one shot (maybe two), but you don't currently know nothing about gymnastics.

This is where the rewinding comes into play. What if you want to play soccer in the World Cup within the next seven years, and you're already thirty-five years old?

When this happens, one does not have to change his or her 7-year vision in the sense that they eliminate the goal. They only have to make the goal possible—attainable. So, cut out the idea of *playing* in the World Cup and instead, set your vision to now read, "I will play semi-professional soccer in seven years" or "I will coach a World Cup team."

Once you've created your 7-month waypoints, put them on your phone as your screensaver.

My own 7-month waypoints, as of this writing, are:

- My food intake is the cleanest it's ever been with little-to-no processed or packaged food.
- I'm in the best physical shape of my life.
- I weight train three to five times a week and do cardio daily.
- My book, *The 7-Minute Setup*, is published.
- I took every opportunity to enjoy family and friends, and make more time available for those who really matter.
- My Facebook Live show is well established and consistent at two to three times a week.
- My content is free-flowing; there are no production issues, bottlenecks, or holdups.
- My workflow for clients is free-flowing; there are little-to-no friction points or bottlenecks.
- The quality of my clients is the best ever.
- I'm helping everyone drive business.
- I'm helping everyone grow personally.
- I help salespeople and management.

They are in random order; a specific order is not necessary. These are simply the things that you're working toward during these seven months. Now, they do have to be in *chronological* order, meaning that I can't have on the current 7-month way-point list "I coach a successful soccer club" if I still think it's legal to move the soccer ball with my hands.

You've got to incorporate the "real" component into the 7-month waypoints as well in the sense that you have to assess whether or not a particular waypoint will take more than seven months to accomplish. Alternately, will it take less than a week? If it will take more than seven months, it will go into the *next* round of 7-month waypoint goals. If it will take less than a week, you can instead put it onto your list of 7-day goals (more on this in a bit).

To return to the Mr. Olympia example, I would perhaps have on my list of 7-month waypoint goals that I'm in the best physical shape of my life and I'm eating properly, because those are two of the first mile markers I need to hit before I can embark on actual competitive bodybuilding training.

This next part is the area where it starts to get a little complicated, but stick with me. This is the point when people have two main objections: *Ohmigod it's too much* (in other words, *I don't want to do this much work*) and *Ohmigod I don't know* how *to do the work*.

When it comes to not knowing how to get started, the issue is one of overwhelm and nothing more. We can handle that. First, take one of your goals and reverse engineer it the same way I reverse engineered the process of becoming Mr. Olympia. If you want to have a house by the ocean, what does that mean? What do you have to do? If you live in Arizona, the first thing you have to do is move. In order to do that, you have to sell your current home. You need to find a new house to move into. You need to have the money necessary to make a long-distance move.

Let's say your goal is to purchase a house that currently costs $1 million. It would be safe to assume that, seven years from now, that house will cost approximately $1.2 million. You may determine that you'll need your current house to be paid off to the point that you have enough equity to leverage in order to qualify for the new mortgage on the $1.2 million house. That means you'll need to make more money in order to pay extra toward your current house each month. Perhaps seven months from now, you want to have an extra $10,000 paid off on your current mortgage. So "I have paid off an extra $10,000 toward my current mortgage" becomes the 7-month waypoint.

By the way, while it seems like everyone has a goal of having a house by the ocean, I do not. I like my house. A lot. On December 4, 2018, I purchased it with my lovely wife, Andrea. It makes my previous house look like a shack (and it was in no way a shack). I like my daily drive to the gym, and on that drive, I have to go through Colts Neck, which is an ultra-rich area of New Jersey full of Wall Street and hedge fund guys. It's loaded with thoroughbred racehorse farms and legitimate mansions. Bruce Springsteen has a house there, so it likely comes as no surprise that the average annual income in Colts Neck is well above the national average.

I drive through it simply because that's the fastest way to the gym. I look at the enormous houses and think, "In a couple of years, I may be able to afford that." But it's not what I want. It's not what matters most to me. Each time I drive through the town, I almost religiously pass four brand-new white Bentley SUVs that cost at least $200,000 a piece. I also pass at least one Lamborghini. And a Maybach. These people are not visiting from Long Island; they actually live here. I'm slumming it, driving through in my Yukon Denali! They probably look at me and think, "Oh, he must be here to fix something; maybe he's Bruce's plumber."

I've attained the level that I wanted to attain when it comes to a home. The house I'm currently living in was on an older 7-year vision. But all of the items on my *current* 7-year vision? I can accomplish all of them while living in the house I'm in now. A bigger house wouldn't make a difference—except that it would add the complication of a larger mortgage payment, which would require that I change things in order to be able to pay that mortgage payment each month. A bigger house would also add increased utility bills. And a larger landscaping fee. And a larger water bill. Overall, it would add an unnecessary layer of complexity and expense.

A few months ago, I went to get coffee at Wawa. Yes, that is in fact the name of a convenience store on the East Coast. As I was stirring this or that into my coffee, I looked over and saw an employee who immediately grabbed my attention, and I immediately wondered, "How many hair nets does that guy have on?" I got my coffee, and as I was walking up to pay for it, I was thinking to myself, "Man, if I had to go to work at a job where I had to wear a hair net every day, that's something I'd really have to push myself through."

I got to the counter to pay for my coffee, and of course his line was empty, so I walked over to his side of the counter. He had one hair net for his hair. And then he had one that went down over his beard. And then he needed another one because of his mustache. And he had to stand there like that in the middle of Wawa. He wasn't even able to hide in the back. He was right up there in front, ringing everyone up. And you know he was standing there fully aware that everybody realized he was wearing three hair nets!

Now, he pushed through this nightmare for one of two reasons. One, he has no aspiration in life whatsoever. This is just a job. His parents told him he can't just sit on the couch and play Fortnite all day and night. He had to do something. So this is what he's doing. Or two, he's got two kids, works nights, and this is how he can make an extra $200 a week so his kids can eat. In that case, perhaps the vision of seeing his child eat is pulling him through his days. Regardless, as a mere bystander, I don't know which reality is his, so there's no point in placing judgment on it. In truth, I had no idea what was going on. But what I do know is that he was either pushing or being pulled to get through that day.

How granular the 7-month waypoints have to be depends on the person creating them. Some people can work with higher-level waypoints, while others will need to break them down into smaller steps. The process becomes more granular in Step 3, which we'll get to...in Step 3.

When it comes to not wanting to do the work, believing that it's way too much to do, my immediate rebuttal is, "Well, you've got seven years." People quickly forget that they don't have to accomplish the 7-year vision in seven months, and when they're reminded of that, the goals don't feel nearly as insurmountable. Listen, you don't make $1 million by just walking outside your front door and tripping over the doorstep into a pile of money. You have to actually do things. You don't just wake up one morning fifty pounds lighter than you were the day before. All of it takes time.

When it comes to doing the work (and, let's face it, sometimes the work sucks), in the end, I know how much I want the outcome. I want that outcome more than I care about the pain of whatever I'm going to go through to get to it. That's the place you have to be coming from as well.

I could say to somebody, "In order for you to have $1 million in the bank, you have to have saved a certain amount per year. In order to do that, you need to earn a certain amount so that you'll have money left over to save. In order to earn that money, you'll have to work. A lot."

Then, they perhaps adjust their 7-year vision to "I have half a million dollars in the bank." I always reinforce that yes, it's hard. But most times in your life when you have done something that was hard, and then it was over, what did you say? You said, "I could have done more" or "That wasn't so bad." You were stronger afterward. As you hit each of your 7-month waypoint goals, you're going to be stronger and stronger and stronger as you inch closer to your 7-year vision. Every time you reach one of your waypoints, you celebrate the small win. You cross that waypoint off the list (with gusto, remember) and you move on to the next.

I think about the #75Hard challenge and the fact that so many people "failed" at Day 62. And they really beat themselves up over it. How many of them instead celebrate that they spent sixty-two days doing hard things they'd never before done (at least not for sixty-two consecutive days)? There's no losing. There's no failing. There is only forward motion. As long as you're moving forward, you're not failing. The only way you lose or fail by doing none of it. Then, it's undeniably a major "L" in the win/loss column. But that's the only way that such a result is plausible.

Another important point is, you may reach one of your 7-month waypoints and think, "I don't like this. This is no good." Perhaps your 7-year vision involves the statement "I am a vegan." Within three months of eating this way, you might hate it. Or, perhaps your body needs the nutrients you've cut out of your diet. At this point—whether it's three days or three weeks or six months into your seven months—you get out your Sharpie, cross off the promise, and rewrite it. You recognize that there's a pivot, and you modify from whatever point makes the most sense. Let's say you discover a medical reason why you can't be 100 percent vegan. You then realize, *I can change the 7-year vision to being pescatarian or vegetarian instead of vegan.* That's a win. It's a win mostly because you've become clearer on what works for *you.* People often dismiss how much of a win that is out of a competitive sense of wanting to accomplish something in the exact same way that the masses are accomplishing it.

Running hurts my knees because I'm fifty. If I realize that fact a week into my 7-month waypoints (within which I declared that I run five miles per day), I'll change the waypoint that says "I run five miles a day" to "I bike fifteen miles a day," because bike riding doesn't affect my knees.

The real beauty of this is that you have the ability to make it flexible and make changes as certain priorities change. You may want to run five miles a day (or bike fifteen) and then, all of a sudden, something happens. A parent gets sick and you have to take care of them, leaving you without the time necessary to exercise to that level each day. Your 7-month waypoint then perhaps shifts to be more in line with your 7-year vision of having a close relationship with your family, making your parents proud of you, and valuing your intimate relationships. In support of that, you swap "I run five miles/bike fifteen miles per day" for "I visit my dad four times a week and run errands for him the other three."

The only thing to keep in mind when adjusting the 7-month waypoints or the 7-year vision is, each of the new waypoints still has to be possible to achieve in the respective timeframe.

The entire process is alive. It will change. It will evolve. And that's totally okay, because you're in control of it at all times.

7-month waypoints help you break down what feels like an enormous vision into more manageable (and reasonable) chunks. Let's say one of the items on your 7-year vision is, "I am working with my favorite HGTV star" or "I am in a successful and enjoyable professional partnership with Mark Cuban." You're not going to slide into Mark Cuban's DMs, say, "Hey, let's partner up!" and find him on your doorstep, anxious to get started. That's not how it works. Even if you meet Mark at an event and have the opportunity to address him directly, it's not how it works.

Gary Vaynerchuk takes questions from event attendees just before taking a photo with them that they will no doubt post on all of their social media feeds. He films the questions along with his answers to use for content because...well...it's great content, and the questions are had by many, so his answer is wanted by many. Once I saw a video of a kid giving Gary his card, saying, "Here's my card; my phone number is on the back and…"

Gary put the card in his back pocket and interrupted him, flat-out saying, "I'm not going to call you."

The kid then said, "If I send you a T-shirt (he was in the T-shirt business), would you wear it?"

Gary said, "Dude, I'll wear it every day, but what *you* need to do is post content four times a day." The point was, Gary knows that simply putting on this kid's T-shirt and wearing it publicly—everyday even—will not launch this kid's business. What will launch this kid's business is taking the time to build his own loyal fan base, which is done through the consistent creation of content that resonates with his ideal audience. This kid (and admittedly, he was really young) was thinking, "The fastest route to success is to get Gary to wear the shirt; it will go gangbusters. Everyone will want one." It wasn't Gary's business advice that he wanted most; it was his perceived spokesperson status.

The way you get to a Gary or Mark or HGTV star to truly partner with you (and, to be clear, I don't think any of them partners with anyone at this point; I'm only keeping them in the example for continuity) isn't to run directly to *them* and immediately ask them to give something to *you*. It's to include as part of your 7-month waypoints the process of *genuinely* getting to know those *around* them. The word "genuinely" is key. You have to have your own standards when it comes to people's behavior. If someone's a pain in the neck, they're a pain in the neck. You don't keep kissing their ass just to get to their boss. Doing so will only put you in the position where you find yourself saying, "I have to do *this* to get *there*? No thanks."

People's intuition is strong. They know if you are "using" them to get to someone else or get something from them. Most of the people you might want to partner with right now have, in truth, zero to gain from working with you. That's just a fact. You need something from them, but they likely need absolutely nothing from you. In fact, working with or in any way endorsing you could actually negatively impact their credibility, which is why so few celebrities endorse anything, and those who do are heavily compensated (with full transparency) to do so.

Some of your 7-year visions may feel like they require that you jump from the north to the south side of the Grand Canyon. Use your 7-month waypoints to build and travel ziplines from one to the other, utilizing the canyon all around you.

Most people reassess their overall goal list in December or January because it's the end of one year or the beginning of the next. When you instead take on this process every seven months, however, your first assessment might be in January. Your first *reassessment* would then be in August. Your next reassessment would be in March. Each time you reassess, you're in a different time of year, which I see as a huge advantage. Some people are so overwhelmed in November and December that it's a terrible time to assess anything, let alone *reassess* anything! Some people get a burst of energy as the spring starts. Some people look at the end of June as the "end of the year" (schoolteachers, for example). Giving yourself different seasons and environments from which to reassess goals will only ensure that those goals are thought through in a more well-rounded manner in the long-term.

After you write out your 7-month waypoints, take a screenshot of the list and make it the home screen on your phone. That way, every time you touch your phone—which, for most of us, is many, many times a day—there it is. Your subconscious will ask you, "What did you work on today? Did you get any closer to these goals?"

Right now, my food intake is the cleanest it's ever been. If I take a look at my list as my screensaver when I'm in the airport and have a fast-food hamburger in my hands, I'll throw that food in the trash.

Bottom line: You need goals that you intend to hit over the next seven months. These are the waypoints that will get you that much closer to your 7-year vision.

3

7-Day Plan

The next step is to identify what you will accomplish over the next seven days in pursuit of your 7-month waypoints. It's important that you plan your week to ensure that you don't drift. You must get in the habit of outlining your tasks for the week *before the week starts*. I plan out my week every Sunday morning, but pick a time that works best for you. Again, write them out on paper. Do not plug them into your phone in a notes app; if you do, you will only lose or ignore the list. I don't title my weekly list my To-Do List. I title it "This Week" or "Next 7 Days."

Seven is the new five; it's not about thinking about a five-day work week any longer. It's also not about shifting to an "I work seven days a week, eighteen hours a day" stance. It's about the fact that, every single day, you choose to do things that get you closer to your 7-year vision.

When it comes to my own 7-month waypoints, examples of accomplishments to put on my 7-day plan are:

- "I have sent an email to the head of marketing for such-and-such company."

- "I have updated my profile on Facebook, Instagram, and LinkedIn."
- "I have investigated gyms to join."
- "I have signed up for a membership at the such-and-such gym and gotten information on hiring a personal trainer."

Perhaps the reason for emailing the head of marketing is that doing so is the second step to partnering with a new company I'm dying to partner with (and I know who their head of marketing is, because finding out was on last week's list). I signed up for a gym membership and asked for information on working with a trainer because I have no idea what I'm doing at the gym, so I know that I need a trainer. Otherwise, I'll just stand there, look around, cry, and leave. So, my written-down accomplishments would include, "I've contacted James Morrison at ABC Agency" and "I've signed up for a gym membership and personal training." You then add to the list any other task you will have accomplished by the end of the week that leads you toward one or more of your 7-month waypoints.

Again, the way you word each goal is important. Don't declare, "I will sign up at the gym and get a trainer." Instead, declare, "I signed up at the gym and got information on working with a personal trainer."

Don't prepare your weekly list in terms of what specifically is accomplished on Monday, Tuesday, Wednesday, and so on. Think instead about what you want to accomplish over the next seven days as a whole. If you have an appointment on Monday to chat with someone about a new client account, write that on the list. This way, you won't forget about this appointment. You'll be continually referring back to the list. Even though you'll likely have the meeting in your phone and on a written calendar (if you use one), you still want to write it on your 7-day plan, because when you write something by hand, it gives it life and makes it less likely that you'll forget (or neglect) to complete it.

Determining how many accomplishments you can reasonably put on your 7-day plan takes a bit of getting used to. If one of my waypoint goals is "I am in the best shape of my life when my birthday arrives in two months," I know that working out is a continual activity. So, in that case, I'd write "I went to the gym five times this week" on my 7-day plan.

You may have accomplishments such as "I called my mom," "I reached out to so-and-so," "I made contact with Jerry," "I closed two deals," and "I wrote 10,000 words of my book" included in your 7-day plan. Once a week, refer back to your 7-month waypoint goals to ensure that your overall 7-day plan is still in line with those. As you get more experienced with this approach, you'll only need to refer back to your 7-month waypoints every two or three weeks.

There may be items that you put on your weekly list somewhat reluctantly because you see them as things you "have" to do even though you don't necessarily want to do them. But, never forget that you have no idea how things will come together for your benefit, and sometimes, you have to allow time for a phone call to assess whether or not something you think has no merit might, in fact, have merit.

In 2003, I almost completely blew off Gary Vaynerchuk. My agency worked heavily with Comcast, and one of their reps called me one afternoon. She said that this young kid had come to her, wanting help with advertising. I asked which dealership he was associated with, and she responded that it wasn't a dealership he was associated with; it was a liquor store.

I asked, "What the hell am I going to do with a liquor store?" and she replied, "I don't know, but there's something about this kid, and he needs an agency to work with. You should at least meet him." She gave me his number. I didn't call him.

The next week, he called me, and because there was no caller ID back then, I answered virtually every call that came in. He said, "Hi, this is Gary Vaynerchuk. My family owns a wine eCommerce website and liquor store in Springfield, NJ called WineLibrary, and the rep at Comcast said that you are the one I should speak to about advertising and marketing." My mental response: *Fuck.*

I didn't want to take time out of my day to talk to him, but I did. Because if someone asks for help, I rarely if ever say no, and the connection was made by a colleague. We set up a meeting, and I went up to see him at his liquor store. The store, which was called Shoppers Discount Liquors back in the day, turned out to have been a store I had delivered to as both a beer and a liquor distributor. I delivered to that store two or three times per week, and without a doubt, a young Gary Vee surely looked at and signed off on my delivery invoice more than once.

Back when I used to deliver there, the store was a small, weathered corner store, but when I went for this meeting, it looked like a huge office building. Since my liquor delivery days, Gary had taken it over. They bought the lot next door and rebuilt the entire building.

During our meeting, he talked about all kinds of crazy stuff like Google AdWords, the website he'd built (that they managed in-house), and the fact that they were shipping wine all over the country, which was becoming a problem because many individual states' Alcoholic Beverage Commissions were getting upset at companies who were shipping liquor with no liquor tax. As a result, those Commissions wanted his liquor store to stop shipping to their states. He was running ads in the *New York Times* and feeling that they were a complete waste of money. He wanted to find a new way to raise awareness of their website and suspected that Google AdWords would be a solid approach. Google AdWords wasn't big in automotive at that time, so I had little experience with it. I took him on as a client and quickly started seeing what he saw when it came to the viability of AdWords, to the point that I started successfully utilizing the platform in the retail automotive space.

He agreed to purchase a billboard at the intersection of Route 78 and the Parkway that cost $12,500 per month, so I knew he was serious about spending money to get his brand noticed—he just wanted to do it in a way that actually worked! He was at the point where he was just trying to figure it all out, one day at a time. When I sent him the first bill, he called and asked, "Why are you sending me the bill?" He thought he'd pay the billboard company and the billboard company would pay my company. He was *that* new to the game.

Gary was a client for six years, at which point he transitioned into the brand he is today, doing less and less with the wine store. When he opened his own media company, the liquor store was *his* first client, so my services were no longer necessary. It's one of the most fun "coincidental" stories to look back on. It's also a reminder that you simply never know what unexpected opportunity might land in your lap on any given day, so begin to look at making time for things you don't want to make time for as an adventure that might just have a very cool outcome.

The biggest challenge with the 7-day plan is...you guessed it...overwhelm when it comes to reverse engineering the 7-month waypoints into 7-day goals. I once again find myself continually reminding people that they have *seven months* to accomplish these waypoints. If you're looking at your 7-month waypoints and notice a goal that is going to take longer than seven months to accomplish, move that particular waypoint goal down so that it's taken on during the *next* 7-month span.

The "real" component of each goal is again important. If I'm 150 pounds overweight, I'm not going to lose one hundred pounds in seven months without getting very, very sick. I could lose forty pounds in those seven months. Maybe fifty. But not 150. I'm also not a doctor, nor do I play one on TV.

The hardest part of the 7-day plan is sticking to it amidst distractions that come from the outside and have a tendency to cut into your day. One has to learn, through consistent practice, how to create a plan that they can succeed at more often than not because they overestimated the amount of time they had available or underestimated the number of distractions that were going to pop up. I do best when I actually *allow* time for distractions. And allowing time for distractions doesn't cause me to end up doing less. In fact, I actually accomplish more of what's on the list by allowing for distractions to creep in. If I am interrupted by fewer distractions during the week than I originally anticipated, I'm able to knock more things off the list (or even add on new things and complete them before the end of the week. Who's to say that on Thursday I don't add six things to the list?). The week isn't over when everything is crossed off the list; the week is over when the clock runs out! If you complete everything on the list by Thursday, simply add more to the list. If you get to Saturday and have four items on the list that truly aren't possible to complete by Sunday, move them to the next week's list.

The other pitfall people face is putting *way* too much on their 7-day plan. I've seen 7-day plans that include "I built a brand-new website" *and* "I wrote a book." You're only setting your-self up to fail with that approach. "I built a brand-new website" is more appropriately placed on the 7-month waypoints list, while "I picked a website template" belongs on your 7-day plan. Your 7-day plan is full of steps *toward* your 7-month way-points. Unless the only thing you're doing in a week is building a website or writing a book, it's not reasonable to have that listed as a 7-day task. Frankly, even if it *is* the only thing you're doing that week, you're more than likely greatly underestimat-ing the amount of time it takes to build a website or write a book! Phrases such as "I started on" and "I worked on" (fol-lowed by a concrete measurement) indicate that you have a manageable item on your list. The minute you add the word "finished," you better be sure that you were already ninety-eight percent of the way to the finish line before the week started!

I've been asked, "But Frank, when have I done enough for the week? When can I celebrate my accomplishments with a beer instead of adding six new tasks to the list?" Practicing bal-ance does come into play with regard to how many more tasks to add once you complete all of the initial items on the week's list. That balance is completely within your control, which is what makes this approach so great. You always have small wins coming, and you absolutely should celebrate them. The whole idea of scratching tasks off the list is about celebrating a small win. At the end of every day, you're crossing off items from your daily list as well as your 7-day list, allowing both lists to continue being whittled down, little by little. You're constantly flexing your Sharpie muscles by scratching items off of the list.

But let's be honest. You're always going to have a list. Just embrace the fact that the day you don't have things on the list, there's a big problem—you're either dead inside, or you're dead period. As long as you're living with purpose, you'll always have something to do. There's almost nobody who's walking around with nothing to do.

How I personally celebrate my small wins depends on the win. There's the celebration that comes from the simple act of crossing something off the list. Then, there's the celebration at the end of each day when I take the piece of paper that the day's list is written on and (enthusiastically) crumble it up and toss it into the trash can. Then, there's the celebration of taking my 7-day list and having so much stuff crossed off of it that it's empty by Friday, so I get to crumble *it* up and throw it away.

Don't discount that an item on your Saturday or Sunday list could be "Get a couples massage with my wife" or "Take my kid to get a Happy Meal at McDonald's." In many ways, this practice is about changing the paradigm of the dreaded to-do list. It doesn't need to always be full of stuff you don't want to do! You put a task on the list because it needs to be done (take your clothes to the dry cleaners) or because you're prioritizing it (delegate a task to someone else in the office). That's the difference between the push and the pull—you're either pushing through or being pulled through your list every day. Everything on the list leads toward or contributes to your 7-year vision.

One of my pet peeves is guys who unconditionally have to watch football all day on Sunday, but also claim that spending time with their wife and kids is important (meanwhile, their wife and kids hate football). I know, you worked hard all week and you want to spend Sunday relaxing in front of the TV watching football; that's fine. But don't then declare that you don't have enough time to spend more time with your wife and kids—because you just spent twelve and a half hours watching football! Don't say that you didn't have time to go to your kid's soccer game on Sunday when the truth is that the Giants were playing the Bengals and you chose that instead. You will never remember that football game. But you'll remember going to your kid's soccer game, and more importantly, *he'll* remember you being there. He'll remember that forever.

The only exception to this—to doing something in lieu of spending time with your family when you claim they are of utmost importance to you—is when you're doing something that *benefits* your family. If you have to work two jobs and the second job is on the weekend and causes you to miss the soccer game, that's different. The priority is obviously making the money necessary to buy the kid's cleats to wear during the soccer game. Beyond that, I call shenanigans.

My oldest son, Frankie, came over a few weekends ago with his girlfriend. It was the first time we'd met her, and she's so sweet. She's also a *huge* football fan, of Green Bay specifically. Green Bay was playing that day against Dallas. I couldn't have cared less, but I put it on the TV for her.

While we worked on dinner, she and Frankie sat and watched the game. But when dinner was ready, they came upstairs and sat down at the table with us for nearly two hours. She missed the entire rest of the game. She made the choice that it was more important to sit and talk with us to begin building a relationship than it was to watch the Packers game on Week Five.

People complain that they have to push through cleaning the house. But that's not entirely true because, in the end, they want to have a clean home for their family. They say, "I have to push through and get the lawn mowed." But they want their lawn to look nice! There's a big difference between that and wearing three hair nets at Wawa. When you're wearing hair nets at Wawa with no real vision for your future, you're *pushing someone else's pull*, plain and simple.

There will be weeks that will end with tasks still on the list, uncompleted. Instead of focusing on the notion that you failed, focus on and celebrate the things that you *did* get done and how much further those got you. Then, take a good look at *why* the things that didn't get completed remain on the list. Did you simply run out of time? Were there outside factors at play that you couldn't control?

Perhaps one of the tasks on your list was to have a meeting with somebody, but they rescheduled on you twice during the week or got sick or their agenda changed. The determination to be made isn't that it's no longer important for you to meet with them or that you failed. It's merely that circumstances changed or situations popped up that were beyond your control.

Now, if you didn't proactively *call* the guy you wanted to meet with all week, then you have to look at why that happened (or, in this case, didn't happen). Was it because you didn't have the time? Was it because you were afraid to call him? Was it because you second-guessed calling him? Or, did your priorities change because you said to yourself, "I don't really want to call him anymore because I actually don't want to do business with that guy." Remember, you have the power to change the list on-the-fly. You can make a change if a task on your list is to have a follow-up conversation with a specific individual, but then you remember that, during the last conversation you had with this person, he was a jerk, and you've decided that you no longer want to do business with him.

There is a person with whom I was supposed to sign a large contract several months ago. I pitched him, and he loved the concept. But the next day he started pushing back on the rate we'd discussed. I had to say, "If you can't see the value in our fees and deliverables, I'm not your guy." I'd written on my 7-

day plan to follow up with him, and then decided the next morning that, if he didn't call me, I wasn't going to proactively follow up. The issue wasn't that I was in any way afraid to follow up; I merely acknowledged that if I have to school a client on the value our agency is providing—not sell him, he was 100 percent sold—it also means I'm going to have to school him on just about everything else. I don't want to have to do that for the next umpteen years that we work together. Just as soon as I made that decision, he called me, and communicated that he was ready to get started.

When you examine the tasks on your list that didn't get completed, identify whether their lack of completion came from a place of empowerment (as in the above example with one of my clients) or a place of fear. If they came from a place of feeling nervous or unprepared or not worthy, it's important to acknowledge that. Do you want to choose to get outside your comfort zone? Or, are you ready to acknowledge that something (or someone) just isn't for you? Will you make the decision that you have an opportunity to grow from this circumstance? Or will you declare, "This is going on the f**k-it list."

If your 7-year vision includes being more adventurous, and your 7-month waypoints therefore include skydiving, and your 7-day plan includes scheduling your first jump, but when it comes time to call, your subconscious says, "You don't want to jump out of a plane, you idiot. What the hell's wrong with you?", you can keep the "I am adventurous" portion of your 7-year vision but put skydiving on the "f**k-it" list and replace it with something else. Snake handling, perhaps.

The List Can Change Quickly

Corey Csakai is a client I work with who's had an incredible experience incorporating not only the 7-year vision but the 7-day plan specifically into his life. He is a chiropractor with a passion for eGaming, and one of the components of his 7-year vision was to be the trainer and chiropractor to video gamers, so to speak.

His initial challenge when it came to the 7-day plan was that he believed that because he's so structured (he works on an appointment-by-appointment basis), he didn't need to write down his 7-day plan. Because of the closeness of our relationship, my exact response was, "Do it the right way. Write that down." I'm (slightly) more subtle with clients I don't know as well. As it turned out, the process of writing everything down caused him to focus even more, and he'll be the first to tell you that it was a game-changer for him (pun intended). It made it so that he didn't forget anything.

I first met Corey when he became my trainer at the gym. I firmly believe that unless you *really* know what you're doing in the gym (and even then, you're taking a risk), it's a good idea to workout with a trainer. When we began working together, I was forty-eight years old.

Corey, who is in his late twenties, is a licensed chiropractor. He was working for a chiropractic practice, and once he began learning the ins and outs of the business side of the chiropractic world, he grew disheartened. Because he'd done a good bit of personal training while in chiropractic school, he started working at our gym as a personal trainer. The whole idea was that he would eventually move his chiropractic practice into the gym; the owner of the gym loved the idea of having someone there who could support members' personal training *and* chiropractic needs. The fact that he is a chiropractor was perfect for me because I used to have all these problems with knee pain. Since working with Corey, I've gotten rid of my knee pain, and now we've moved on to shoulder pain. But we're working on it.

When you're working out with someone, you inevitably end up talking, and it wasn't long before I discovered Corey's passion for eGaming—to the point where he's figured out a slew of ways that these guys, who are professional gamers (which has become such a legitimate career it's mind-boggling; some of these guys are making millions of dollars and have endorsement contracts, sports agents, the whole thing) can extend their careers and perform better when it comes to their reaction time, posture, and strength.

I suggested that he build an online course around the concept, and the look he shot me said, "No idea where to even start on that one." It seemed as good a time as any to ask if he wanted me to walk him through The 7-Minute Setup. I told him to go home and write out what his life would look like seven years from that day.

Of course, he wanted a big house by the ocean. Beyond that, his list included declarations such as "I am the leading training authority in the gaming industry," "I have helped multiple big tournament winners," and "I'm an established influencer in the eGaming industry. He also stated, "My chiropractic practice is as big as I want it to be," which I found quite interesting. He wasn't committing himself in that moment to a practice that would have a certain financial value or a specific number of clients. He was clearly stating that it would be as big as *he* wanted it to be. He also has complete control over his time.

We then began to talk about what he would need to do over the next seven months in order to move toward those goals. He said, "There's a tournament coming up in eight months or so in Atlantic City." I informed him that he was going to be at that tournament.

"What am I doing to do there?" he asked.

"I don't know," I said, "but we're going to figure it out."

We talked it through and determined that it would be great for him to be at the event, sharing tips and treatments for the participants. I suggested that he get himself aligned with some of the top gamers to encourage them to share his posts or shout him out on Twitter, which is one of the more popular social media platforms for gamers. He started following people, commenting on their posts, and providing tips and value. He let them know he could help them with their reaction time, their muscle cramps, and their postural issues.

Within forty-five days or so, he had connected with two of the biggest gamers and begun providing them with tips and strategies. He then reached out to the company that was running the event (it was a large HALO tournament). They offered to give him a booth at absolutely no cost—a booth that would normally cost about $5,000. The booth was positioned right next to the main stage, so he sent out a slew of tweets and personal messages to the top gamers, letting them know that they could come by his booth for complementary treatments. He ended up treating around eighty competitors. Thankfully, he'd brought two of his chiropractor friends with him to help him with treatments as well as a third friend who worked as a sort of promoter, standing in front of their booth and letting people know what they had to offer.

He ended up getting interviewed live on the Twitch feed right from the tournament for (ironically) seven minutes or so.

There were likely close to a million people watching that feed, and he got seven full minutes of exposure. From that, he got an insane number of targeted new followers, from individual competitors to entire teams. After that tournament, he was invited by the promoter of that particular event to attend the Call of Duty tournament in February 2020 in Las Vegas.

Since then, he's created his own app, which consists of a series of games designed to increase one's reaction time and finger flexibility. The games provide finger workouts that absolutely impact these gamers' reaction times as well as make them less likely to get finger cramps right when they're about to shoot the winning shot or goal or whatever they do.

You might think he partnered with a super expensive developer to get this done, but he didn't. He actually found someone on Fiverr who helped him for under $1,000. He'll upgrade if and when he deems it necessary. For now, however, the app is working very well for everyone involved. He also made sure that his website has a lot of great content on it to attract new followers.

One of the most interesting aspects of Corey's journey, in my opinion, is that while we were working on his 7-year vision, he had some pretty heavy stuff going on in his life, stuff that was starting to bring him down and slow him down, and had the potential to create real havoc. But because the The 7-Minute Setup had him so busy building the life he envisioned, he was distracted enough not to focus any more than necessary on the heavy stuff.

Today, he's treating and training members at the gym as well as working with eGamers on the side. He's ridiculously busy. And happier than he's ever been.

As for where to *put* your 7-day goals once you've written them out, there are certainly options, but make no mistake: the list of goals should be with you at all times. In my case, I've created a planner that has my 7-year vision, 7-month waypoints, and weekly list on one side and then each day's tasks on the other side. It's portable enough to take with me everywhere I go, and if I want to refer to it while on a plane or update it at any point throughout my day, I know exactly where everything it is.

4

7-Hour Workday

Regardless of what you want to accomplish, it will take time, and the amount of time it will take is almost guaranteed to be longer than you initially estimate. Remember the last time you decided to organize the garage and estimated that it would take an hour? Five hours later, you were putting the final containers of holiday ornaments on the shelf. Remember the last time you thought, "I'm going to write a book this year!" Nine months later, you were on sentence number four.

Great news: seven is the new eight when it comes to hours in the workday. For some people, that comes as a massive relief since they're used to a sixteen-hour workday. But let's be honest, most people who brag about grinding for sixteen hours a day aren't spending the majority of their day on the grind; they're spending it on the 'gram.

Your new workday consists of seven *total* hours of real, focused work. To be clear, this does not include time spent watching hilarious cat videos or engaging in mindless Facebook or Instagram scrolling. It doesn't have to be seven hours in a row, and you don't have to start at 4:00am. Many "experts" will claim that you have to start working at 4:00am in order to be successful. They probably eat at Red Lobster and skydive too.

I work much more successfully from about 11:00am until I go to sleep at night. Early mornings are not good for me when it comes to productive work. This has been getting better since I've gotten in better physical shape and have been eating healthier, but I'm still in my best zone after 7:00pm. I can work until super late and still be sharp, hence the reason my Facebook Live show is most often streamed at 9:00pm EST. I'm lucky that 9:00pm EST is prime Facebook viewing time, but even if prime viewing time were at 9:00 in the morning, I wouldn't do my show then with any level of frequency because it would be horrible.

What matters most is whatever works for you.

There is no reason to be super rigid about this part of the process. The point is that working toward your goals needs to consume a solid amount of your time and your being. One of the biggest misconceptions I hear is that those seven hours of goals-focused time have to *all* be work-related. That's simply not true. They're all related to the 7-year vision and the 7-month waypoints, but they may or may not all have to do with your career. If you're managing a challenge with your kid and he or she needs extra attention, perhaps you need to focus on your job for less time each day so that you can invest more time into your kid for a week or two.

If one of your 7-year visions or 7-month waypoints is "I have a really strong relationship with my family," maybe you need to allot two hours of focused time on Wednesday to being fully present with your family—no cell phones, no TV. That time absolutely counts toward your seven hours!

My book editor has a daughter who was born in Ethiopia. A huge priority for her is her daughter's hair and skin, because they are important to her daughter's sense of self (and, as a Caucasian woman, she has exactly zero experience with African hair care or hairstyles, so this priority necessitated a good bit of research on her part). When she adopted her daughter, she vowed to provide her with the best life possible, which included having confidence in her appearance and a strong sense of self-worth.

One day, she learned that the current month's issue of *Essence* magazine was entirely devoted to African hair. She therefore added "I went to Barnes & Noble to purchase this month's copy of *Essence* magazine" to her 7-day plan. Purchasing the magazine for her daughter contributed to her 7-year vision of raising a self-confident young woman who's aware of the sorts of hairstyles she likes and doesn't, which products are best for her hair, and other African-American women who are making a strong contribution to their communities and the world at large. It wasn't a random errand—it was a purposeful errand that was in line with one of her waypoints, which is to be cognizant of what her kids love and what's important to them. This particular waypoint supports her 7-year vision to raise strong, confident kids who know how much they're loved as their own unique selves.

I certainly don't want anyone timing themselves in order to force themselves to a rigid 7-hour structure. The 7-hour time frame is slightly "loosey goosey"—obviously there are some days when you'll work for seventeen hours, and others (when you're sick, perhaps) when you'll work for one. On the longer days, those seventeen hours may include travel, sitting at the airport, sitting on the plane, going to try to find the rental car place, and trying to find the hotel at 1:00am in a city you've never before visited. All of that counts, because it's what you need to do to show up for the meeting that will move the needle overall.

Some people refuse to travel for business unless it's during traditional business hours. They demand that their travel time be between 9:00am and 5:00pm because that's the only time that they're getting paid for. If they're supposed to be at a meeting on Wednesday, they insist on scheduling their travel during the workday on Tuesday. And then again during the workday on Thursday. This means that three quarters of their day on Tuesday and three quarters of their day on Thursday are wasted. It's completely wasted time.

Part of the deal is recognizing that getting to the out-of-town meeting on Wednesday means that you have to put in your time on Tuesday in order to get everything accomplished that you can. It may mean that you need to travel from 6:00pm to 11:30pm on Tuesday so that you're in Tulsa on Wednesday morning for a 9:00 meeting, fresh and ready to go.

"Engage in a 7-hour workday" is really just another way of saying "You need to do what you need to do when you need to do it." You'll average it all together, and it's going to wind up that you're putting in, on average, seven hours of *real* work every day. And if you don't—because you think, "I'll only travel during business hours"—then you're not getting it done. It's that simple.

So many people make things that should take only an hour take three hours to accomplish because they delay, they ponder, they don't focus. They start and stop and start and stop and start all over again. They announce, "Oh wait, I've gotta pee" (sometimes via social media, because in addition to the photos of the massive burrito you're eating, that's definitely something your friends and followers both need and want to know about). Then, they stop and talk to people in the break room between the bathroom and their desk. They go outside for a cigarette. Each time they do this, they need fifteen minutes (at least) to regain the momentum that they had before they got distracted. It's no wonder that in 2017, Piala, a marketing firm in Japan, began giving non-smokers six extra vacation days per year after an employee complained that all the cigarette breaks (in a country where smoking is still deeply ingrained in the culture) were greatly affecting productivity!

Approaches like the Pomodoro Technique, developed by Francesco Cirillo in the late 1980s, can be extremely valuable—especially if focus isn't yet your thing. You get rid of all distractions (phone, notifications, TV, lists scattered all over your desk) in order to work for a solid twenty-five minutes, and then you take a five-minute break. After four rounds, you take a thirty-minute break. There are apps for it and everything (of course).

I don't care what you have to do—set a metronome on your desk and don't allow yourself to stop what you're doing until it tick-tocks 1,500 times if necessary. Seatbelt or duct tape yourself to your chair for a period of time. Do what you have to do to put in the amount of time necessary to get that stuff done. Put your phone on Do Not Disturb. Close the sixty-three internet tabs you have open. Stop looking out the window.

Consider young athletes who will one day go to the Olympics. Take a swimmer, for example. He (or she) will be in the pool every morning at 5:30. They'll put in their time, go to school, and then go back to the pool. They train twice a day, and on the days when they don't have school, they train three times.

It's not about working fourteen hours a day for the sake of working fourteen hours a day. But, as Gary Vaynerchuk says,

"If you're going to bitch and complain about your life, and then you're going to spend the weekend watching entire seasons of 'Game of Thrones' or 'House of Cards,' go fuck yourself" (I'm paraphrasing, but I'm pretty sure that quote was real close to what he actually said, and I agree with it). You're always choosing what's important to you, and the excuse "I don't have the time for that" is an excuse. You have the same amount of time everybody else does. You just choose to do something else with it because that something else is more important to you right now. And, by the way, that's okay—as long as you're owning it! I just gave you permission to go watch an hour's worth of cat videos on YouTube. All I ask is that you not complain to me next week when nothing about your business or life has advanced.

A great analogy when it comes to truly doing the work—truly putting in a solid 7-hour day—came to me one morning when I was working out. When you're working out a certain muscle or muscle group, you often work that muscle to the point of failure. What winds up happening as you get close to that failure point is, there's a transmission from your brain to your muscle that says, "Stop! Put the weights down." That message is simply your brain's protection mechanism ensuring that you don't hurt yourself. But, if you're in control, you know that you can keep going, and as you do, the muscle you're working will start to uncontrollably shake. When that happens, you know you've hit the point where you're *really* working the muscle. You have to then retrain your brain each time you increase the amount of weight you use for that exercise. You "master" a certain weight, increase the weight, feel the shake, get to the point when the shake stops, and increase the weight again.

You can't fake the shake.

If a trainer is working with somebody who says, "This is really heavy," and the trainer looks at that person's muscle and sees that it's not shaking, it's clear that the weight is not, in fact, too heavy. You simply can't make your bicep shake the way it does when you've worked it to maximum capacity, when you're one rep away from failure. The shake is a completely unconscious movement.

In your 7-hour day, you have to train yourself to get to the point where your concentration is so intense during your work time—whether you engage in twenty-five-minute sprints or two-hour blocks—that the "shake" dynamic comes into play. Again, all seven hours are utilized equally. You can sit at your desk for sixteen hours and get the same amount of work done as someone who sits down for two hours and deeply focuses. Once you understand the concept of "hitting the shake" after a focused period of work, you'll know you've done it because you'll feel "the pump."

There's a YouTube video in which Arnold Schwarzenegger talks about this concept of "the pump." (This YouTube video is Frank-approved viewing.) Let's say you do a set with ten reps of bicep curls, and you start to shake around rep number six. When you get to eight, you might fail. Or you might barely make it to ten and then fail. You reach a point at which that muscle simply won't work anymore. When you stop lifting, that muscle is replenished with fresh blood, and you feel what Arnold refers to as "the pump." The muscle feels expanded because it's got so much blood going to it. He compares the sensation to being high, but it's like a swelling—a good swelling, not a painful one.

At the end of the workday or a dedicated work period, you should feel "the pump." You should feel that sense of satisfaction, of seeing the list and each item on it that you've scratched off. I sometimes feel "the pump" when I cross off a big item from the list, even long before the end of the workday.

We were recently working on the website for an auto dealership, and it was a bear to take apart and rebuild. When it was finished, I scratched that task off with such vigor that I absolutely felt "the pump." It was like, "This thing is done, and it looks awesome, and it's gonna perform like mad." You can't make up that feeling. It's impossible to fake.

When you complete a task on your daily plan, cross it off, and cross it off with authority. Feel the pump. I like to use a Sharpie to cross items off of my list because it's bold. I don't put just one line through it, either. I scratch it out aggressively, as a celebration of the accomplishment. It's like I'm telling the task, "Yes, I did this; you're done."

This is what it looks like to live a life that's not about mediocrity. Earlier in the book, I mentioned that there are people out there (a lot of them) who are quite comfortable living a mediocre life. Hell, *I was one of those people.* Back when I lost my business and went bankrupt, I could have gone either way. I could absolutely have settled for mediocrity. Even before that, given that my parents came to this country in 1967 with no education, no English, and no economics, I could have simply continued to tow that line. Their whole focus was simply to survive. I could have adopted that mentality and run with it (or, more realistically, sat on my couch with it).

Growing up, I wanted to work in the car dealership, like my dad. I wanted to be a mechanic, like my dad. I could have easily just done that and stopped there. Or, I could have gone back to it after my business crumbled. Instead of wearing three hair nets at Wawa, I would have rotated between three pairs of rubber gloves in the underground oil changing pit. I could have been just fine and made a good living fixing up pickup trucks while listening to songs about how beer was the only thing that never broke my heart.

But I didn't.

You can decide to spend your days fixing pickup trucks and then go home, watch TV, and go to bed. You can also decide to read a few chapters, make a phone call, update your resume (and, these days, your social media profile), meditate, and go to bed. Each set of choices requires the same mental bandwidth, yet an entirely different 7-year vision.

5

7-Minute Setup

Your 7-year vision is realized month by month, day by day, hour by hour, minute by minute, choice by choice. Just as the journey of one thousand miles begins with a single step, the journey to the realization of the 7-year vision begins with the daily 7-minute setup.

It should take you no longer than seven minutes every single day (or the night before) to plan out the day ahead. If it takes you longer than that, you're putting way too much on your plate, and you're not going to accomplish the majority of it. Then, at the end of the day, you're going to look at it and say, "I can't ever finish anything. I'm such a loser."

I've found that if I plan my day the night before, as soon as morning comes my focus is primed and I'm ready to go. For me, it seems to be easier to set up tomorrow the night before because everything that I need to do is fresh in my mind. I'm looking at the list from the day that just ended to see what needs to be transferred over to the next day, and I also have my "This Week" or "Next 7 Days" goal list nearby.

There are four concepts that I've found to significantly increase the traction gained from a strong execution of The 7-minute setup:

- Have flexibility.
- Hone self-discipline.
- Get more frank.
- Go one layer deeper than you normally would.

Have Flexibility

There is an important need for flexibility and awareness with this daily list. You might have twenty-three things on the list, and twenty of them will take less than five minutes each, while the other three will each require an hour or so. You might have just one item on the list that will take you a full seven hours. The number of items truly isn't what's important; it's about getting a sense of a day's manageable workload so that you're setting yourself up to succeed. I still often move items from one day to the next, and I also have days when I finish everything on my list by 2:00pm and then add more. The point is that you have a plan in place for your day—that you allow ample time to complete the big items and don't forget about the small items, like checking in with someone, making a doctor's appointment, or putting a fifteen-pound turkey in the oven before 4:00pm.

It's a skill you hone over time through practice. You have to let go of the notion that having more on the list is better. If you have only one item on your list for the day because you know it's going to take the full seven hours, that's okay! Look at a surgeon's schedule, for example. If he has to perform a seven-hour surgery, he's likely not going to add rounds or another massive surgery onto the end of the day. He'll delegate those tasks to a partner in his practice.

Some time management experts recommend that you get your biggest item out of the way first. Others recommend that you take an hour to get all your three-minute tasks completed so they no longer take up mental space. I was brought up (professionally, anyway) on the Franklin Planner, and therefore, the way I prioritize my list is based on what absolutely needs to get done on any particular day. With that in mind, it's really more a matter of personal preference whether you first dive into the big-ticket item or cross the little things off the list so the list feels more manageable. Regardless, the goal is to get everything completed while not beating yourself up if you happen to underestimate the amount of time something will take or have an unexpected interruption in your day that requires your attention.

One thing I am extra cognizant of is identifying whether there is a task on the list that I need to delegate, and if so, getting that finished first thing in the morning. I can't save it until the end of the day, because if I do, I'm giving the person to whom I'm delegating it little-to-no time to do it. If I know I have a call with someone at 8:00am, and I know I have a few items that have to be delegated, I make sure to create the time to do that delegation *before* the call, even if that means starting my day earlier than initially planned.

Hone Self-Discipline

Flexibility is important, but you also need to employ a certain amount of self-discipline combined with common sense in order to recognize "I need to do this first because I need to hand it to somebody else" or "I have a doctor's appointment at 11:00, and the doctor's office is an hour away. I need to leave the house by 10:00 no matter what so that I'm not late to the appointment."

When you make your daily task list and know you have too many items on it to reasonably complete in a day (and this will happen more often than the alternative), you must simply prioritize by asking yourself, "What's more important? What do I *really* have to do?" The items that are of lesser importance or less critical to the accomplishment of the overall 7-day plan can be moved to the next day.

If you are an entrepreneur who's currently wearing a lot of hats (and by a lot, I mean all of them), I completely understand how overwhelming and tedious this list can feel from time to time. From project proposals to bank account reconciliation to increasing the WiFi speed to communicating with customers, the list can feel long and unwieldy. At some point, many (if not most) entrepreneurs are ready to pass a hat (or seven) to someone else, and while they've dreamed of the moment when they could do that, they find that it's a very hard step to take when the moment arrives. They've learned to trust only themselves, and "It'll take less time to just do it myself" becomes an all-too-common statement.

When it comes right down to it, what's critical to acknowledge is how important it is to get the list tackled. You'll probably have to fail more than a few times at that and suffer the consequences of doing so—either because you don't have the requisite skills to do a task quickly and with quality or because there are only so many hours in the day—before you accept that the best route is to admit that it's time to delegate a particular task or train someone else on how to properly complete it.

People often wonder exactly when it's the right time to start delegating certain tasks, and my belief is that it's the right time when the pain of continuing on the same way becomes too unbearable. Come to think of it, one has to feel more than just pain. In order for any pivotal change to be undertaken, one has to reach a certain level of outright disgust—with themselves, their life, and the things around them that they could control, but don't.

While it introduces an entirely different (and equally important) topic, one about which a number of other books have been written, it's important for me to note that the degree to which The 7-Minute Setup method will create change in one's life has a direct correlation with his or her level of self-awareness. If you're not aware of your own strengths and weaknesses, you'll learn to be aware of them (or in full denial of them) quite quickly. If you remain in denial of them, things are going to keep falling apart around you. You'll have a solid 7-year vision, and you'll probably have solid 7-month waypoint goals, but your 7-day plan and daily plans will be clumsy, at best.

Get More Frank

Self-awareness has many levels. At the point when most of us think we're as self-aware as we could ever be, there are probably three (or ten) more layers waiting to be revealed. It's a lifelong process, and it's a critical component of The 7-Minute Setup method. After all, the vision you're shooting for will be more aligned with who you authentically are at your core the more self-aware you are; the roadblocks keeping you from reaching your vision can most easily be removed the more aware of yourself you are and the more honest you're willing to be with yourself.

In that moment when I was sitting on the balcony in Wildwood, New Jersey thinking, "This has to change, and the change has to come from me," that newfound level of honesty came from the recognition that I was addicted to drifting. Drifting is easy! To be clear, the reality of living a life where you're constantly drifting is not easy at all—buying SPAM by force for dinner is not easy. But blaming everyone and everything else for the fact that I couldn't get my life together? That was easy. That's the route whereby you don't need to exercise *any* self-awareness or take *any* responsibility. You just walk around blaming somebody or something else, ever the victim.

In my case, there were a few scenarios that continued to repeat themselves. One, I was constantly running out of money. I didn't have the money to pay bills, and I had people from the utilities companies, the credit card companies, and the trash collection company calling me and demanding the money I owed them on a monthly basis. At one point, of course I blamed other things—not other people, per se, but other circumstances—for the fact that I kept running out of money. But there came a point when I was able to acknowledge the faintly whispering notion that the common denominator was always me and my bad decisions. Once that faint notion starts to make its way in, that's the beginning. When you're completely closed off to it, it has no chance of creating change. But once it gets your attention—even the slightest bit—it can start wiggling its way in more often and more deeply. That's when real change begins.

There are people who will live their entire lives believing that whatever issue they're dealing with at any given point isn't theirs. There are others who will, at some point, whether after the first time they go broke or the fiftieth, have a moment where they say, "Oh my God, this is all my fault." Some of those people will take one or two steps in the right direction, meet resistance, blame something outside themselves (boss, co-workers, customers, spouse...) and blow up that progress (or the progress will get blown up because the job will be lost, the relationship will then suffer, and the dominos will fall fast from that point). Others will get a small win and use that win to propel them forward. They will encounter a setback and use it to learn something about themselves so they don't end up in the same situation the next time. Their self-awareness and growth continue to build upon one another like the steel beams of a skyscraper.

The path is different for everyone. Some may have that critical moment after hearing a specific quote or a song on the radio, or after reading a paragraph of a book that resonates with them. Some may have it after a day or a week in the woods with no technology. Some may have it while walking to the mailbox. Regardless, to all of a sudden realize that everything you have and everything you are—good, bad, or somewhere in between—is 100 percent your fault is, without a doubt, a humbling moment. For most people, it's also a very painful moment and not one that any normal person would necessarily *want* to go through. That's why we tend toward drifting—to avoid that moment entirely.

Once you can make peace with it, however, it becomes an extremely empowering point in time. You recognize that if you had the power to get yourself wherever you currently are, you also have the power to get yourself wherever you want to be.

You don't have to rely on somebody else giving you an opportunity or validating your idea by writing yourself a blank check. You can go make your own magic. You can create your own opportunity. There are so many people on this earth that the odds of pulling oneself out of the mess they're in are in everyone's favor. The planet is so congested that no matter how badly you've screwed up in the past, you'll eventually run into somebody who doesn't know that you are (or were) not a nice person. You may have burned 4,867 bridges, but lucky for you, there are at least 8,386 more out there! Unfortunately, many unsuccessful businesspeople use this fact to their advantage to steal from more and more people.

My greatest advice is to be real and—pun intended—to be frank with yourself and with others at all times. Every time I wasn't, it bit me in the ass. It's the way I express myself at all times, unless I sincerely don't want to hurt somebody's feelings. That said, I'm noticing as I get older that it's easier to be frank with anyone and everyone because I just don't care anymore about politeness when I know someone needs to hear something in order to better themselves or their situation. The fact is, if you're true to yourself, if you're consistently frank with yourself, you'll keep yourself out of a whole lot of trouble and save yourself a tremendous amount of time. You won't waste time because you will always be on the right wavelength, in your truth. When you're in frankness with yourself, you can say, "This is the way it is, and let's fix it. Let's make it right. Let's make it better."

If someone says to me, "Frank, I'm tired. And I'm going to sit on my couch today and watch Netflix," I'll first ask them if that's what they really want to do. As long as the answer is yes, I'll say, "Cool!" But if they do that consistently and then end up complaining to me about their circumstances, I'm going to respectfully remind them that they spent all those days on the couch watching Netflix. If I blatantly shame them, I'm a jerk. On the other hand, if I respectfully point out a reality they can't argue with a straight face, it strongly encourages them to take ownership.

People spend far too much time defending their choices and wanting those around them to co-sign those choices. In the end, you can do whatever you want to do. But there's a logical consequence to the choices we each make, one way or the other. Don't complain about having to cook dinner for forty-three people on Thanksgiving when your boundaries weren't strong enough to say, "I want to have Thanksgiving with only my significant other and my kids this year." If you do put up that boundary and your Aunt Carol gives you a hard time about it, Aunt Carol can go to her sister's house for Thanksgiving.

Otherwise, you're going to cook for forty-three people, including your Aunt Carol, and you'll have to accept that you put yourself through that. You have to be frank with yourself that making Aunt Carol happy above making yourself happy is the choice you're making. Perhaps part of your 7-year vision will be to create better relationships with your extended family so that, seven years in the future, you can invite forty-three people to Thanksgiving dinner without wanting to put your head in the oven before noon.

It's also important to get frank with yourself when it comes to the amount of pride you're carrying. I've seen people's pride take center stage at this point in the game and badly hold them back. Perhaps, in the short term, you have to choose to go work at Kohl's for eleven dollars an hour, even though you're forty-four years old with a Bachelor's Degree in English, and your new manager at Kohl's is a twenty-seven-year-old named Mohli (but pronounced Molly) who never finished high school and criticizes the way you put used hangers in the used-hanger bin when you're working on Black Friday after hosting forty-seven people for Thanksgiving.

If you're self-aware enough to know *why* you're working at Kohl's on Black Friday for eleven dollars an hour, telling Mohli with a genuine smile that her approach to used-hanger management is brilliant—why didn't you think of it?—you can get through it. You can be pulled by your vision.

I have a friend who is so resistant to ever again working in a sterile cubicle for someone she doesn't respect on a project she's not passionate about that, in order to make ends meet, she has vowed that she would drive for Uber or Lyft or whip up lattes at the local coffee shop for all the people heading to their jobs in a sterile cubicle each morning before she'd go back into one herself simply because it "sounds" better and doesn't hurt her pride. Her boss at the coffee shop would likely be thirty years her junior, but she'd let her vision pull her through, knowing that every single day she'd have the opportunity to meet and talk with interesting people, having no idea when one of them might offer her the opportunity or the tip of a lifetime.

During a trip to Richmond, Virginia, I used Uber to get to a meeting. My driver, Eduardo, was from Venezuela. Having owned a trucking business in Venezuela, he and his wife had come to the U.S. several years prior due to the political challenges in Venezuela. They settled in Richmond because his wife had family there. He didn't want to start a trucking company in this country because doing so would be too expensive. Instead, he started flipping homes. He never took out a loan on a home (he always paid cash), and he didn't like owning more than one at a time; he'd purchase one, renovate it, flip it, and then use a portion of the proceeds to invest in and renovate the next one.

I asked him why he drove for Uber, and he said that there were two reasons. One, he drove his wife crazy if he was at home too much, and two, driving for Uber was one of the tools he used to find (or sell) his homes. At that point, he'd sold two of his homes to passengers and had learned about five that he ended up purchasing while chatting with passengers who were locals and knew of someone selling, or getting ready to sell, a house.

Most people (and I was part of this bunch at one time) can't suck it up and make lattes or organize hangers or drive other people around for a bit because they don't see it as a part of the (much) bigger plan. They're living too much for right now and too strongly identifying with their current inability to get out of the "thing" they're stuck in. They walk around simultaneously believing that they're going to live forever and die any second. They're pushing from both ends, being pulled from neither, and can therefore accomplish next to nothing.

Now, if you're reading this book, you are already, on some level, ready to look in the mirror. You can't be any more ready than you are in any one given moment, but I trust that you will continue to increase in your readiness, one realization and choice at a time.

The first thing to get real honest with yourself about is that you have the potential to do more and to do better. I'm not only referring to your bank account balance. You must acknowledge that, even if you're still figuring it all out, you have everything inside you that you need to be where you are *and* get where you're going.

Second, you have to be honest about how badly you want the change. The idea of living in a big house by the ocean may initially excite you, but the bare truth may also include the fact that you really don't want to leave your double-wide trailer or garden apartment. If that's the case, own that, and stop complaining about every single aspect of your life. Openly and wholly enjoy your trailer or garden apartment!

Think about people like Eduardo who purchase old houses with the intention of renovating and flipping them. They buy a house that was built in the 1940s, and based on initial inspection, establish a renovation budget they're excited about. But three weeks in, the contractor identifies a previously unseen issue with the foundation or the need to remove and replace the entire HVAC system. And then, the new owner loses his mind and starts blaming all sorts of things and people—the contractor, the inspector, the realtor—for not seeing an issue that wasn't able to be seen until the roof was removed and the walls were torn down. All of that blame is misplaced and a complete waste of time. It's not any one person's fault, necessarily. You bought a house that was built in the '40s and then forgot that you needed to plan for things to not go as planned—because you bought a house that was built in the '40s! You make sure that, to the best of your knowledge at the time, you have the best realtor, inspector, and contractor working with you. And you also plan for the unplannable. And then you figure out, with your trusted team, how to best address the unforeseen issue. If you discover that someone isn't a good fit for the team, you find gratitude for that new understanding and work on finding the right person.

You have to be prepared for the worst thing that can happen. If you're not willing to accept and manage the absolute worst thing that could happen in a certain situation you're considering going into, don't go into it.

When it comes to a DIY renovation, I can only assume that the worst thing would be termites or a bad roof or a bad foundation (or all three). If you're not willing or strong enough to handle any or all of those possible realities, if you can't manage the idea that you could rip down the sheet rock or tear the plaster off the walls and discover four generations of rats or cockroaches or termites camping in there, don't buy the house to begin with. It's that elementary. Everything in life comes with risk. I take a risk every day when I walk to the mailbox—one of those white Maybachs from Colts Neck may be lost, driving 150mph trying to get out of my neighborhood while responding to a text from their stockbroker and end up permanently taking me down, right there next to my mailbox. If you're not willing to gamble on something, just don't do it. But also, quit complaining about your life.

When my parents came to the United States, they played a very conservative game, just like most immigrants did. They didn't spend a lot of money. If they didn't absolutely, positively need something, they didn't buy it. If anything in their foundation cracked or fell apart, they had limited resources to address it. Those facts created a limited base from which they could start over and reinvent themselves if they needed to. This is why so many immigrants come here and kick ass—there's no going back, so they come here, work really hard, and spend *no* money.

While plenty of immigrants came here, opened a business, and worked really hard, plenty of others didn't. They just weren't willing to risk what they already had. Maybe they didn't have the necessary self-confidence, maybe they didn't have the resources, maybe they didn't feel they had the overall depth to be able to withstand an unforeseen crisis. Instead, they got as much as they could out of working the way that they worked, while knowing their life was still so much better than the life they came from.

In all honesty, when making a job change or a relationship change or a geography change, what is the very worst thing that can truly happen? I find it interesting how many times we hear people say, "Thank God I didn't know it was going to be this hard; had I known, I wouldn't have done it." Ignorance is bliss to a degree, and you do have to be a little bit out of your mind to take some of the leaps and have some of the dreams many of us have. But at least we all understand one another.

So many people ask me about my own employment situation, about why I don't go out and open my own agency again. Put simply, I'm self-aware enough to know that I'm not willing to risk all of the benefits that I currently have. I'm not referring to medical or retirement benefits. I'm referring to the fact that I don't have to care about who takes lunch when, or who's mad at whom in the office. I have a lot of freedom to grow the business in a way that I deeply enjoy, and being the sole owner of the company is not worth the added stress that would come with the assumed prestige of being in that position.

The place people have to get to in order to be able to take that first transformative step (and continue to take steps, even when it gets tough), is the place where they declare, "I'm miserable. I'm sick of this. And I'm the only one who can get myself out of it." Until you get to that point, lasting change won't happen.

In one way, I don't want to put that prerequisite out there because it sounds a bit dramatic. But I know I have to. Sometimes people are in the place of "Give me anything new. I'll try anything new." But they're impatient. So, they try something for a week and don't generate their million dollars or have their perfect partner or their beautiful house by the ocean. They then decide, "This approach doesn't work. I quit." Other people, however, can be at it for only a week, get a micro win, be satisfyingly fed by that, and build on it. Everyone is different. Many people will mask the real reason something doesn't work by saying, "I tried it for a whole week; it doesn't work," when the reality behind that statement is that they didn't really want the thing in the first place, so they blame the fact that they didn't get it in a week instead of owning the realization that they didn't actually want it at all.

It's like going on a date with someone and recognizing before the appetizer has even been delivered that the person is crazy. You don't want to see them again, but you do because you're desperate to be in a relationship. And then, six months later, you end the relationship because...wait for it...they're as crazy as you assessed them to be from Day One.

Let's refer back to a previous statement: "If you discover that someone isn't a good fit for the team, you find gratitude for that new understanding and work on finding the right person." This could also apply to going on a first date with someone who is clearly psychotic.

Go One Layer Deeper

I once worked with a client who desperately needed to release an employee from their duties (which is a nicer way of saying, "They needed to fire them. Immediately"). This person was incredibly toxic to the overall environment and was contributing absolutely nothing to the bottom line. In fact, on some days this person was clearly sabotaging business opportunities, even if unknowingly, and draining everyone of their emotional resources on a daily basis. I directly told the client, "You *have* to fire this person."

His response was, "I know that, but I just don't want to blow things up."

Newsflash: things were already blown up! And they were continuing to blow up every single day this person came into the office and did (or didn't do) their thing. Further, sometimes you have to simply tear off the BandAid; otherwise, you're simply engaging in a longer-term process that is far more painful and time-consuming but has the same end result. The real question in this case wasn't, "Why hasn't this person been fired?" It was, "What unknown 'thing' are you so afraid of happening and how on earth could that be worse than what you're presently dealing with?"

If you aren't someone who likes feeling as though you made a rash decision, add the phasing out of this kind of employee and the hiring of a more suitable team player part of your 7-month waypoint goals. Incorporate that goal into your weekly (and then daily) lists of interviewing new prospects, having an honest conversation with the current employee, and, one way or another, moving forward instead of staying stuck in the limbo of hell. The limbo of hell is comfortable because it's familiar. But it's hell. So get out of there.

6

7 Seconds of Reality

Y ears ago, when I started to practice the 7 seconds of reality, it monumentally changed my life. Every single morning, when you first wake up, you must fill your brain with gratitude. I once told someone this, and he looked at me and said, "I don't know what to be grateful for. What's good?" The minute I heard those words come out of his mouth, I started to cry. And, of course, I had to ground myself really quickly because in order to truly help somebody, you can't cry for thirty minutes in front of them!

I said, "Well, how about, number one, you woke up?

Because so many people did not. Number two, you woke up with your mind intact. You woke up knowing where you were. Many people wake up and don't know where they are. Number three, you got up out of bed, because you are able to. Many people are not."

When things are tough—and as mentioned, I have absolutely been in this place—it's the most critical time to employ this part of the process. For some people, starting their days with a 7-second "reality check" is a precursor to creating their 7-year vision, and that's perfectly fine. Any time life starts to feel overwhelming or challenging, when you wake up in the morning and your first thought is, "Is it time to go to bed yet?", bringing your focus back to your 7 seconds or reality is a sure-fire way to get out of the thick of despair as quickly as possible. These are the moments when this practice best flips one's perspective.

At many times in my life, I've woken up and immediately wondered how many hours had to pass before I could climb back in bed and go back to sleep. The reason I felt that way was that being asleep was better than experiencing my waking reality. When I was asleep, I didn't have to deal with anything.

I remember a time when I was in one of the worst depressions of my life. It was late 2010 or early 2011, and things were really, *really bad*. I was seeing a therapist, and he'd say to me, "Frank, you have to look to the future, not the past." This was during a time when, if I heard the song "Yesterday" by The Beatles, I would just break down. Wherever I was, I'd have to run somewhere like a bathroom where I could be alone to uncontrollably cry like a baby. There's a line in the song: "I'm not half the man I used to be," and thinking about it can make me cry right now. I had such a longing for the way things used to be—the way *I* used to be—and the line would repeat in my head over and over again. The therapist I was seeing would say things like, "The future is better. You have to focus on the future; you have control over that. The past is in the past, it doesn't matter."

My response was: "Well, what do you do when the past seems better than anything that could come in the future?"

I don't remember his exact response to that question, and I'm sure it wasn't positive, but over time, I realized that the reason I thought that the future couldn't be better than the past was that I wasn't looking at my future properly. I was thinking that my future was always going to be the same as my present, and that I didn't have control of it because I believed that I'd lost all control over my life. I believed that if my present continued the way it was, my best days were already behind me. And this is a really sad way to think when you're only forty or forty-one years old—to stomach the idea that your best days are already behind you. In my case, I had lost everything, and I didn't believe that I could build it again or that I could replicate it—or better it!

Beyond intense depression, another reason people wake up and immediately want it to be bedtime is that they're aimlessly drifting through their life. As such, they're in a constant reactive mode that starts the second their eyes open in the morning. They wake up, get the kids ready for school, get themselves ready for work, realize there's no gas in the car, get stuck in traffic, identify a different route to avoid the traffic (or just sit through the traffic), get to work, discover that their email inbox is full... That's what it looks like to exist in reactive mode, and it sucks. It doesn't constitute an intentional, purposeful, focused life. To be fair, from the moment many of us wake up each morning, a lot of the above-mentioned activities *do* go on! But you can take all those things and recognize them as intentional components of your 7-year vision. When part of your promise to yourself includes having kids who you know are living the best life that they possibly can, who are fulfilled and thriving, you know that those kids need to get to school. From that perspective, getting them ready and taking them to school is not seen as a chore. You're then off to work and trying to save money to start a side business or invest in a family vacation (some vacations are an investment!). With that perspective, going to work has a purpose beyond just paying the bills.

One day I was driving by a random cemetery, and in a split-second, as I observed the lines of headstones, a thought came to me: Every one of the names on those headstones was a person at one time, just like me, just like you, living their life and doing their thing. Maybe that life was good. Maybe it was bad. Maybe they had some joy in there, maybe they had a lot of joy in there. But whatever it was, however it played out, it was over. There was no chance of them feeling any of those feelings of pain or pleasure, success or failure, excitement or fear, pride or shame ever again. Also, there's a certain amount of time that's going to go by after which no one will remember them at all. One's life just falls off.

In reality, there are only a few handfuls of people whose names the masses know: George Washington, Gandhi, Napoleon, Mother Teresa… Their legacies continue. But one day, even their legacies will lessen. Like, who was the fifth emperor of Rome? Nobody knows, right? You have to look it up. During the six seconds when you're looking it up and acknowledging the answer, that guy (Claudius, whose full name was Tiberius Caesar Augustus Germanicus, for the record) has a life that once again matters. And then, four minutes later, when you've once more been captivated by your Facebook feed or the nonsense otherwise going on around you, it's gone again.

Time. It's the one concept we can't go around, under, over, or through. No matter what, time will get every one of us. Maybe a little sooner, maybe a little later, but regardless of what Michael Buffer declares at the end of any boxing match, the absolute undisputed champion of the world is time.

These are the 3 A's with which I start every single day: Alive, Aware, and Able.

Alive

It's very simple: You woke up again today and thereby got the greatest gift of all. And you get it over and over and over again during your life—the ability to be alive, right now, in this time period, with all these other people, with all of this technology and these conveniences and opportunities at your fingertips. Given that scientists estimate the odds of you being born to be around one in 400 trillion, the fact that you're alive is fascinating in and of itself!

Aware

My mother is battling Dementia and Alzheimers. She wakes up each morning but can't do much past that point. Everything that happens from the moment she wakes up is simply a bonus. She forgets what her purpose is and what she's supposed to be doing. And that truth has made my father *extremely* aware, because he's taking care of her. Truly, the fact that your brain is working and you are aware of who and where you are is such a blessing, because obviously, it could go away.

The awareness that you've woken up, that you're not dreaming anymore, that you know who you are and that you have a list of things to do, people to see, and people depending on you allows you to stop seeing the day solely as being "full of tasks." The kids depend on you to take them to school because if they don't go to school, they're not going to get an education. The school depends on you to bring the kids to school because it's their job to teach the kids, and if the kids don't show up, the whole system falls apart—there's no one for the teachers to teach! If you don't go to work, the customers and clients who depend on you to answer the phone when they call are left hanging. This principle holds true even if your job is as "menial" as being a janitor. If you're the janitor, everybody in the facility depends on you for certain things, and the minute something goes wrong, everybody loses it. With little warning, the janitor, custodian, maintenance guy, whatever his title, instantly becomes saint-like the minute whoever is in charge needs the toilet to stop running or the lights to be turned back on or the water to be cleaned up off the floor so no one slips and cracks their head open.

I remember talking about the basics of The 7-minute setup concept several years ago when it was still forming in my mind with a friend named Joe Ocello. He was a porter at a class-A commercial office building in New York City, and one day he said, "I see this guy who is the head of the maintenance department rolling up in his nice car. I want to be that guy." Imagine my surprise when I recently saw one of Joe's Facebook posts with a photo of him—now the maintenance manager of a huge college apartment complex—making significantly more money. He's now in the position he previously aspired to. Four years ago, he was cleaning toilets, a step ahead of miserable. But through the power of networking, defining his goals, and having a solid plan, he's now happier than ever. And he accomplished this in less than six years.

It really doesn't matter what it is that you want to do. It doesn't matter how seemingly unattainable your 7-year vision is. Nor does it matter where you are now. You just need to put a process in place that will get you there.

Able

Yes, there are people whose bodies no longer work, but thankfully their brains still do. They can still communicate. That's the extreme end of the spectrum, but let's say something happened to you physically; perhaps you broke your leg and were in the hospital. You might be able to work from your hospital bed, but the situation would slow you down. I think about how often the older generation says, "I've still got my health!" and it really is a critical awareness for them, given what they want to do with the rest of their time here on earth. They want to be independent for as long as they can. "She's going to fall and break her hip" has almost become cliche, it's said so frequently of older people, but many of those older people are genuinely terrified of breaking a hip because it's such a difficult injury to come back from physically.

These are the three categories with which you start your 7 seconds of reality each morning. While it's important to have a bit more of a minimalist attitude when it comes to your 7-month waypoints, your 7-day plan, and your daily tasks, your 7 seconds of reality needs to be a *minimum* of seven seconds, but it can go on for as long as you'd like. Here are some additional A's I like to consider first thing in the morning. You can add as many items to the list as you want—*after* Alive, Aware, and Able. After all, if you're dead, none of it matters, right?

Ability

Ability is different from "able." Ability refers to the skills that you've acquired over time. Whatever basic knowledge you've received over the course of your life will stay with you forever. For example, once you learn to ride a bike, you'll know how to ride a bike for the rest of your life.

Whenever I emcee or keynote a conference, I begin by congratulating everybody for being there. Whether someone was able to attend because somebody else paid for his ticket, or he bought the admission ticket with money from his own pocket, there will be a monstrous return on the investment that will last the rest of his life. Most people take that moment to look at me like I'm crazy because it often seems unlikely that one conference can provide insights or approaches that will continue to positively affect someone for the rest of their life. I remind them that the knowledge that they'll get and the people they will meet and the opportunities and connections that will arise as a result will stay with them forever. Also, they didn't have to be at the conference. They could have stayed home and watched "SpongeBob," but they're not going to remember that episode—unless it was a really good one.

Associates/Anticipation

You have associates who are anticipating on a daily basis the actions you're going to take. In other words, the fact that people depend on you indicates that you're needed and valued. These associates anticipate that when they pick up the phone and dial your number, you're going to answer. They anticipate that when they send a text to you, you're going to read it and reply. They anticipate that if they send you an email with a problem, you're going to send back an email with a solution. Hell, if you're the person who makes the morning coffee in the office, they're anticipating that you're going to complete that mission *and* make sure there's unexpired creamer in the refrigerator.

Your associates can include your family members, your friends, your colleagues, and your co-workers, for starters. It's whomever you come into contact with on a daily basis. At our local grocery store, Wegmans, there's a really kind older gentleman who works at the deli counter. If Andrea doesn't go to the store for a few days, when she finally shows up, he asks, "Where have you been?" It's usually been only a few days or so since her last visit, but he anticipates that she's going to come by at least once a week for her weekly order of items from the deli counter.

If you're someone who goes to Starbucks every morning on your way to work and you skip a day or two, when you pull up to the drive-thru window three days later, the barista may say, "I've been wondering where you've been!" She anticipates you showing up each morning. You're a part of her consistency as much as she may be a part of yours. Even if you break that consistency all the way down to the person who goes into Starbucks every morning and pays with their Starbucks app, if they decide to hand over cash one day instead, the cashier's head might seem to explode with confusion as they ask, "Don't you want to use your app for the rewards points?"

Anxiety

Every single person I've introduced to the 7 seconds of reality—especially if they battle any level of anxiety—has told me the exact same thing: It gives them control over the anxiety that can show up at the beginning of the day. The fact is, you can't feel both gratitude and anxiety at the same time.

The basic premise of the 7 seconds of reality practice is to make the feelings from your conscious mind stronger than those from your subconscious mind. Your subconscious is where anxiety and/or depression come from. It's the origin of the stupid, broken record in your brain that says, "My life sucks. I don't have this or that anymore. I don't have my yellow Lamborghini, and I'm never going to get it back." From that moment, you begin an endless spiral of putting yourself down. That's the momentum with which you start the day, and it's all downhill from there (and not in a good way).

Habits take time to break, so for those who wake up and immediately begin to ponder all of the reasons they're already anticipating bedtime, my suggestion is to set up the alarm on your phone differently. On most devices, when you set an alarm, you can title it. You could title your alarm ALIVE / AWARE / ABLE. Or, 7 seconds of reality. As soon as the alarm goes off, the first thing you'll do is grab your phone; you have to look at it in order to snooze or stop it because the days of slapping a snooze button are long over. When you look at it, you'll immediately see ALIVE / AWARE / ABLE displayed.

The truth is, the first seven seconds of your day are extremely volatile. If you're in deep, deep depression mode, those seven seconds are actually bliss because of the fact that you

aren't yet fully aware that you're awake. In your brain, you remember that the last thing you were doing in your dream was
flying a fighter jet shooting at Nazis or something. For me, I'm
flying a fighter jet and I have Jerry from "Tom and Jerry" with
me. He has his headphones on, and he's making shooting noises
with his mouth. Because he's a cartoon.

That time—the span of just a few seconds—is absolute bliss.
Because your subconscious doesn't yet realize that you're
actually awake, you feel no anxiety, no pain, no anything.
You're just good; everything's good. And then, all of a sudden,
your subconscious realizes that you're awake, and it turns on
the shower of anxiety.

Have you ever fallen asleep on the beach near the shoreline,
and as you were sleeping, the tide started to come up and all of
a sudden you were hit with a wave? That's how I describe the
way anxiety used to wash over me the moment I was aware that
I was awake. I would instantly go from being totally fine to
having that under-the-skin muscle shake that you can't
control—because "you can't fake the shake," remember? From
that point forward, I was playing catch up to determine what I
could do to get rid of that awful feeling.

Just like a muscle, the harder you work your mind in terms
of having consistency with this practice, the stronger it (and
you) will become. Your momentum will only continue to build
each time you engage in the practice. It will get to the point
where, when you first wake up, you're in the gray zone, and
then, *bam*, you automatically start on your 7 seconds of reality.
After a while, you'll have generated so much momentum that
your previous first-thing-in-the-morning anxiety won't stand a
chance.

In the beginning, you may have to engage in this practice
for more than seven seconds each morning. If, on a scale of 1

to 10, your anxiety is at an 11 one morning, you may need to do it for fifteen or twenty minutes. I call it 7 seconds of reality because what you're noticing and paying attention to truly is *reality,* and it only takes seven seconds to realize the three A's. You're alive; that reality is undeniable. If you're able, there's no disputing that fact. That is your reality, not the made-up stuff that your brain has trained itself to believe—that you're not good enough, that you're a failure, that you have all this stuff to do, that you hate life, that you hate your wife or husband, and on and on. You start with what is absolute.

I'm working with a young woman right now who drastically suffers from anxiety, and the 7 seconds of reality practice has thoroughly transformed her life. It set her up differently to the point where she was starting her day in the right frame of mind, and that allowed her brain to generate the necessary momentum to properly place all the pieces that appeared throughout the day.

Another client of mine was a personal trainer, and he wanted to be a professional fitness model. The 7 seconds of reality was huge in his life because he too suffers from anxiety. When he doesn't engage in this practice, his brain starts off the day "stuck," and it only gets worse from there. The 7 seconds of reality is how he "primes the pump" for the day.

7

Crew of 7

It's commonplace for some people to listen to everybody. As in, people in their circle, people *not* in their circle, the grocery store clerk whom they've never met, and perfect strangers at the park. They take advice from everyone they ask (and they ask *everyone*), and then they change direction like a confused mouse in a maze based on the way each of those people advises them. I've watched someone take eleven completely different suggestions from eleven different people—and none of them is even remotely in line with where they're trying to go.

Unintentionally listening to everyone is a symptom of drifting. All you're doing is being whipped left and right like a windsock. Additionally, some of the people you're talking to are telling you things that's for their *own* benefit; their focus is on what they can get out of you as a byproduct of you making the choice they're suggesting!

Your crew of 7 is extremely important. You don't *have* to have seven people, but you can have *no more* than seven. If you do, you've got gibberish going on, and your wires are undoubtedly getting crossed. There are too many cooks in the kitchen, as they say. More voices than seven is simply noise. And noise doesn't give one clarity or forward momentum.

Your crew of 7 is comprised of those people you have made feel safe enough to be able to tell you anything—whether good or bad—if it's something you need to hear. When they're sitting next to you and you're watching "The Bachelor" while complaining during commercials that your book isn't finished, this is the person who will respectfully call you out. If it's something that they believe they need to say to you to support your growth, you've made them feel safe that they can say it to you without you taking them out at the knees in response. The flip side of that is that you feel safe listening to whatever advice or thoughts they're providing because you know that they only have your best interests in mind. They don't have a dog in the fight beyond wanting you to succeed.

You have to be able to confidently confirm why the person you're speaking to doesn't want you to fail. For example, you must be able to say, "You don't want me to fail because you tried this exact approach, you know it won't work, and you don't want to see me end up in the same position you ended up in." That's very different from "You did this and failed, and now you don't want me to do it because if I succeed, I'll show you up."

When I first honed in on the concept of having a crew of 7, I quickly recognized that I had some people in my own crew who often gave me advice based on what would most benefit *them*, not me. Sometimes, what most benefited them was me *not* succeeding, because if I were to succeed, it would only make them more aware of their own shortcomings or how little they had evolved over the years. That person cannot be part of my or your crew of 7.

You must be confident that each member of your crew is going to give you input or advice from a place of genuinely caring about you—not because they have anything to gain from you beyond receiving the exact same thoughts and advice in reciprocation. That should be the only exchange: you're both in each other's "crew."

The relationship does not, however, *have* to be reciprocal in terms of your role in each other's crew. You might consider someone a part of your crew who doesn't consider you part of theirs, and vice versa. That's okay! You may be part of someone else's crew, but they aren't a member of yours because they're too focused on themselves, or they're too busy, or they just don't care.

If you have zero people in your crew right now, that's perfectly fine. You get to build your crew intentionally over time. People tend to worry about exactly where and when they'll find their crew, but trust me, they'll come once you start intentionally working on your 7-year vision. When all of your actions are in line with your 7-year vision, your "people" will begin to find you. They'll be working on their own promises to themselves and their own visions, which may look completely different from yours, but the point is that they're putting the same energy out there.

There's a line in the movie *Coming to America* when Eddie Murphy's character, Akeem, asks his barber, "Sir, where can one go to find nice women here?" Arsenio Hall's character adds, "We've been to every bar in Queens."

The barber responds with, "Well that's where you messed up, son. You can't go to no bar to find a nice woman. You got to go to nice places, quiet places, like a library...or a church." Just like the barber advised, you have to put yourself in places where there are good people. There are jerks everywhere, but there are more jerks in certain places than in others, because there are places where jerks congregate—like strip clubs. And Red Lobster (I'm kidding). You're probably not going to find your crew of 7 in a strip club; you're only going to find jerks there.

If you have people in your crew today who suck, get rid of them so you can create room for the ones who are going to help you move forward. You don't have to cut someone off completely or be a jackass about it by posting a formal announcement on social media that so-and-so has been cut from your crew. You simply acknowledge to yourself that they aren't someone you are going to go to anymore for professional or personal advice. Or, maybe they're good for personal advice but not professional. Or the reverse. You simply have to know what the boundaries of the relationship are and alter your behavior accordingly.

For example, when you're feeling bored, you don't go hang out with your drinking buddy, Rusty, at the bar anymore. Instead, you read a motivational book or watch the Tony Robbins documentary on Netflix. Or, you throw a ball against a wall over and over again. Because almost *anything* is better than going out with Rusty, getting hammered, and being useless the next day. But that doesn't mean, however, that if Rusty calls you and says, "Hey, what's up?" you respond by saying, "Screw yourself." You just politely decline when he invites you to go out and get hammered.

Your crew will connect you with the right people at the right time, without even realizing it. One day, Dylan, the twenty-three-year-old I met at the gym and gave the Grant Cardone hats to—asked me to recommend some people for him to follow on social media in order to keep his newsfeed full of good stuff that he actually wanted to pay attention to. I gave him a bunch of names, and I threw Joel Osteen in there.

I said, "Matter of fact, he's going to be in New York this weekend." Dylan said, "Well, I'm gonna buy a ticket. Are you going?" We had been thinking about going, so long story short, I bought tickets for Andrea, our son Preston, and myself on Friday night. Preston is a big Joel Osteen fan. He makes Andrea put him on in the car every morning on the way to school. He likes the positive messages going into his mind in the morning, and I think he also likes the fact that, if he's listening to it, Andrea can't talk to him about the fact that he needs to clean his room.

Dylan was texting me during the event, saying, "This is absolutely life-changing, and I'm so happy I'm here. The power in this room is amazing!" Afterwards, we were all in line to meet Joel, and Dylan was in front of my family. He went to shake Joel's hand and pulled him in closer in order to say something to him privately. He had his head down, but he was speaking so loudly that we could all hear him. He said, "You need to know that, before a few days ago, I had no idea I was coming here. And the reason I'm here is because of that guy right there (pointing to me), who I didn't even know a week ago." Joel thanked him for coming, they exchanged a few more words, and that was it.

Preston and Andrea said hello (Preston made it a point to tell him how much he enjoys his jokes while he listens to him on the way to school each morning), and then it was my turn to shake his hand. I said, "Hey, I'm Frank Lopes." He grabbed my hand, pulled *me* in, and said, "Thank you for delivering your friend and your son here tonight." I said, "You're welcome. I'm just trying to keep the good stuff in their minds."

Not only can you get great advice and guidance from those in your crew, you can also glean a lot of beneficial approaches to life and business. I have a good friend named Damian Boudreaux who I met at a conference that we were both speaking at a couple of years ago. I was speaking on Day One; he was speaking on Day Two. I instantly knew that there was something unique about him. Almost immediately after meeting me, he asked, "What do you see yourself doing in the future?" He was more interested in what I *wanted* to do than what I was actually doing (assuming those two things were different).

Damian does an incredible job of very quickly turning a conversation around to the point where he's not talking about himself but instead asking about the person he's talking to. I've become more conscious of doing that myself, as talking about myself really isn't very exciting. As quickly as I can, I'll turn the conversation from someone's initial question about what's going on with me to what's going on with them.

Another of Damian's talents is that he has no problem cracking someone open like an egg. I've seen him do it to multiple people; he'll start talking to you, and the next thing you know, he's in your head, as suddenly as you hear the sound that's made when you tap an egg on the side of the bowl. But, after he cracks you open, he doesn't just let you spill all over the place like Humpty Dumpty. He cracks you open in an effort to help you realize that you can become a better version of yourself as well as to identify what's really holding you back and hurting you and what your real obstacles are. He cracks your shell with the hope that it will allow you to take a good look inside and do something amazing with whatever you see in there.

One thing I hear people say when someone in their circle is on the brink of success is, "Don't forget about us little people when you get big!" That's a bright red flag that they don't in-tend on evolving much from where they are presently. There's not anything necessarily wrong with that if where they are makes them happy, but it's an indicator that a particular person isn't going to be someone who has your best interests of evolv-ing in mind, because they aren't on the same path.

Sometimes people around you will give you grief for not spending your money on certain amenities. For the most part, those people are simply trying to feel better about the fact that they wasted their own money on those things. On the flip side, some people will look down on you for what you *do* spend money on, like a personal trainer, a Ritz Carlton vacation, or a monthly subscription to a cigar club. In this case, they don't have the money to invest in those things, so they don't want anyone else to be investing in them either (or, at the very least, they don't want people to feel good about the fact that they do invest in them). These people are not part of your crew.

I committed to slowly building a crew that would support me and encourage my growth. I knew that, perhaps after a cou-ple of years, there would be some flux and flow in the members of the crew because everybody's agenda changes. Everybody's constantly evolving. As such, they have traits that put them in your crew (or vice versa) at one point in time, and then, as things in their world evolve, they may evolve past you (or you may evolve past them). It's not about evolving *above* someone else, it's about evolving in such a way that your paths no longer align well enough for you to be in their crew or them to be in yours. Subtle changes to your crew can actually serve as a great indicator that you are, in fact, growing!

I reassess the members of my crew every time I chat with one of them. Somebody could say or do one thing that rubs me so massively the wrong way that I'll think, "This person has evolved in a different direction." It's also important to recognize that there may be people who are sort of "part-time members" of your crew. Some members will be more consistent than others. Some will be called upon more often than others.

This past December, Andrea and I went to see renowned opera singer Andrea Bocelli perform. As we listened to the magnificent performance right alongside thousands of others—the venue was completely packed—it occurred to me that, because Bocelli is blind, he doesn't know what that packed venue looks like. He's never seen—through his eyes—the difference between ten people, one hundred people, or one thousand people listening to him perform. When one or more of someone's senses is compromised, the others are heightened to compensate. Even though it's not officially categorized as one of our five senses, intuition is absolutely a sense, which is why it's often referred to as our sixth sense.

I don't know which of Andrea Bocelli's senses are most heightened in response to his lack of sight, but I have to imagine that his "BS" meter is pretty high. When he meets an adoring fan, I have to imagine that, based purely on the way they sound and the way their energy feels, he can tell rather quickly if the person is genuine or not, and to what degree.

For those of us who have our eyesight, it's important to remember that our eyes can deceive us, so we can't always trust them. Instead, listen to the words someone is saying and the tone they are using. Let the way something makes you *feel* direct your decisions rather than the words themselves or the story you might tell yourself about the words they are saying. Just because something looks good doesn't mean that it is. Also, if you're ever feeling challenged in your ability to be self-aware, just close your eyes for a moment. Look inward using your internal eyes—your intuition—in order to stop yourself from thinking, "I'm not [fill in the blank] enough to [fill in the blank]." Remember, whether Bocelli gets in front of one person, 20,000 people, or 100,000 people, he always performs at his best.

A Critical Disclaimer

N ow that we've covered the last of the seven steps included in The 7-Minute Setup method, there's a critical disclaimer I need to set forth before you go out into the world and begin doing your thing.

**Do what this book says to do,
but don't be a jerk about it.**

People get on these all-or-nothing bandwagons. They claim that in order to be successful, you have to write down your goals three times a day for a year, keep a gratitude journal, and handwrite "I am victorious" five hundred times every month. They go on to declare that if you don't do all of those things, you won't find the level of success you seek. Listen, if you see someone who's drifting, I promise you that's not the kind of direction they need. They might do all these things after you tell them to because they get that initial burst of "Hear Me Roar" adrenaline, but as quickly as that adrenaline rush hits, it will wear off. After that, they'll only do these exercises mindlessly (if at all) just to check the box next to "do something new...anything at all." People evolve in different ways. If someone isn't using the exact system or method someone else has prescribed, it doesn't mean that they're out of touch or fifty feet behind the ball.

My wife is a health coach. She helps people get their nutrition and lifestyles on track. There's a breakfast item she puts on her clients' menus that contains sweet potatoes. Most people fall in love with this recipe; I did not. I do not like sweet potatoes. But when she heard this, she didn't say, "You're an idiot, Frank. Just eat the goddamn sweet potatoes. That's the way it works." Instead, she said, "Okay, we'll swap it out for raspberries." She didn't delete the entire recipe from my menu; she modified it so that it worked for me.

When people get on a kick to do things differently, it doesn't take long for them to get "motivation muscles." They start following Daymond John or Gary Vee and almost instantly start criticizing and putting down everybody around them who isn't on the same thought train. If some or all of someone's strategies resonate with you, that's awesome. But don't assume that they are the right strategies for everyone in your circle as well.

It's easy to tell when someone has newly developed motivation muscles. These are the people who "deejay" too much. Most actual deejays don't make much (if any) of their own music. They're not always musicians, but to a degree, they're creators, given the way they take other people's music and put it all together to create something new. I see people who deejay one person's (or a bunch of other people's) content way too much. The only time that they say something with their own voice is when they're criticizing someone else for not being on the same page they're on.

The fact is, those with newly activated motivation muscles are quite comfortable quoting everyone else, but they're terrified to use their own voice. They wear other people's philosophies and perspectives as their own muscles, and they don't fit. They're trying to become Tony Robbins or Joel Osteen by proxy. They're not comfortable or confident or creative enough to come up with their own quotes, so they use someone else's. And then, in order to put themselves in a position of perceived power with pretend confidence, they shame everyone else.

If someone is constantly quoting a specific expert and telling members of their circle that, if they aren't doing it the way that person is doing it, they aren't going to be successful...run. It's seemingly the same philosophy by which some people become doctors. It's not about helping others; it's about having been bullied as a kid and wanting the power to say, "Your gallbladder needs to come out, and I'm the best person to do the job."

Maybe someone gets nauseous at the idea of thinking seven years in the future. That amount of time may feel too overwhelming. They may instead want to think about the seven months, seven days, or seven hours ahead. But that person can still use all the principles and jump in and out at any time. You can jump into the deep end or the shallow end of the pool. If you want, you can run and cannonball into the deep end, swim to the shallow end, and walk up the steps onto the concrete deck. Or, you can walk down the steps one at a time, slowly getting each body part used to the water before you swim to the deep end, grab onto the side, and push yourself up and out of the pool. You can use this method in any way that you want. And, if you don't do every single option exactly as directed—if you decide to slowly immerse yourself in the shallow end, swim to the deep end, and then climb up the ladder to exit more gracefully than you would if you tried to hoist yourself out—it doesn't mean that you suck.

One day, a client called me and said she was struggling with something and needed to chat. Her dad is a bit...shall we say...difficult. He had lost his job, and he was trying to find a new one, and my client was giving him all these books by Tony

Robbins and Zig Ziglar—the same books she read, books that had inspired and motivated her.

I quickly had to stop her. I said, "You have to understand something: Your dad's not in the same mindset that you are, nor is he going to be. You're saying that he's not helping himself because he's not going on Indeed.com to find a job, and he's not knocking on doors. But that's not him. That's not the way he's going to tackle this challenge."

She asked if she was a bad daughter for not paying her dad's mortgage, and I said, "No, and to be honest, your father probably doesn't want your money. Has he asked you to pay his mortgage?" (He hadn't.) I asked, "Has he asked you for money?" (He hadn't.) I communicated that she was creating unnecessary static between her father and herself. Now, if her dad had said, "I really need to update my resume, and I don't know how to do it. Could you come over with your laptop and help me add the details of my last position to my resume?" and she said no, *then* perhaps she wasn't being the most supportive daughter she could be. If the computer isn't his thing, and she knows how to use it but doesn't help when he asks, that's not being supportive. However, if he doesn't follow *her* specific execution plan on how to get a new job, that doesn't make him a bad or undetermined person. Maybe he wants to go get the newspaper and look through it the same way I did in 1994 after our trip to Wildwood, New Jersey. As I explained to her, she had all these motivation muscles from what she'd been consuming, but she couldn't use those muscles to put her dad in a headlock! That wasn't the right thing to do. You can't force your beliefs or advice down anyone else's throat. They have to sit down at the table and say, "I want to try this." *Then* you can throw it in a pan, warm it up, and serve it to them.

Part of the reason people with newly formed motivation muscles end up acting like jerks is that they need validation. They think, "Okay, I'm going to adopt this new process, but if I can't get everybody else on board with it, maybe it means I'm crazy for thinking it might work."

You don't need to convince anybody else that what you're going after or the way you're doing it is okay. You just need to just be comfortable and confident that what you're going after is what you actually want in seven years' time.

I saw a social media post recently about a guy who went to the home of another guy who's very successful, financially speaking. As he walked through the home, he noticed that there were no TVs. So he went home and immediately removed all the TVs from his own home, as though that shift (made in a vacuum) would make all the difference—without understanding exactly *why* he was removing the TVs and how that would benefit his own trajectory. Beyond announcing in his social media post that he'd done this for himself, he went on to state that anyone who has TVs in their house doesn't *really* want a high level of success. This is asinine. Anyone who says, "If you have a TV in your house, you aren't a real entrepreneur" or "If you watch 'Game of Thrones' you'll never be successful" is a jerk.

On the other hand, if part of your 7-year vision is "I am in the best physical shape of my life," your first set of 7-month waypoint goals may include something along the lines of "I have lost ten pounds." In order to accomplish that, your "This Week" list may include, "I ate healthy meals each day," "I exercised five days this week," and "I got enough sleep every night." If you're falling asleep every night to the late, late, late, late show, *that* may be a good reason to take the TV out of your bedroom! But that's completely different from saying (to someone who undoubtedly didn't ask for your opinion on the matter to begin with), "If you have a TV in your bedroom, you're not a real entrepreneur."

Conclusion & Next Steps

Through the course of this book, I've detailed The 7-Minute Setup method, the method that I've found to be extremely helpful in my own life and that of my clients, friends, and associates. While it's a step-by-step process, you must first and foremost, *get clear on where you are,* because without being honest about where you are, it will be impossible to create an authentic 7-year vision or the proper path to get you there.

Regardless of where you are right now, regardless of where you've been, you have complete control over where you're going.

While I utilize all seven steps of this method and I encourage you to do the same, please remember that *something* is always better than nothing. Running might be faster than walking. But walking is faster than crawling (which is faster than sitting on your couch eating Cool Ranch Doritos). If it feels too overwhelming to take on all seven steps of this method right away, pick one! Contemplate your 7-year vision, or take just one aspect of your 7-year vision—health or relationships or career/impact—and focus on that first. Or, start considering your crew of 7. Or practicing the 7 seconds of reality. One thing I can promise is that when you stop looking outside of yourself and start looking *inside*, you'll get clear far more quickly than ever before on what you really want. Once you know what you really want, that knowledge provides all the motivation you'll ever need to take the next step...and the next...and the next.

There are *so many* things that you *can* do, be, and achieve in this life. But most people will get caught up in the things they believe they can't do—to the point where their focus only holds them back and they end up doing nothing. We all know somebody like that. Don't be the person who comes to other people's minds when they think about who that person is in their own experience. You can get out of your own head, get past the limiting beliefs, and get to the goals and the vision you imagine. It is my great hope that The 7-Minute Setup will be the method that allows you to prove this to yourself once and for all.

You deserve an incredible experience in this life—and you have within you everything you need to create whatever you need to create in order for the rest of your life to be the best of your life.

It's now time to close this book, count to seven, join us in the engaged and growing 7-Minute Setup Community on Facebook (www.Facebook.com/groups/7MinuteSetup), and get on your way! Remember, you have everything within you that you need to make the rest of your life the best of your life.

Frank J. Lopes is the Vice President of FB Digital, one of the automotive industry's hottest digital marketing agencies. Frank currently leads and guides the marketing efforts of some of the largest volume and fastest growing automobile dealerships in the country.

Frank has been quoted in various national publications, including *Fast Company*, *INC*, *Capital One Spark*, *Dealer* magazine, *Dealer Marketing* magazine, and *Dealer Solutions* magazine. He is also a regular contributor to automotive-industry related podcasts and news shows.

A prolific keynote speaker, event emcee, and dominant presence on social media, Frank spreads a message of positivity and growth to his followers. As a mentor and personal coach to members of the automotive community nationwide, he speaks out on controversial issues facing the automobile industry and is an evangelist for positive change and the customer experience.

www.GetMoreFrank.com

www.Facebook.com/TheFrankJLopes

Twitter.com/TheFrankJLopes